THE CHRISTMAS COMPANION

A merry little book of festive fun and trivia

Sonja Patel

THE COMPANION SERIES: COLLECT THEM ALL

The Birdwatcher's Companion
by Malcolm Tait and Olive Tayler

The Cook's Companion
by Jo Swinnerton

The Countryside Companion
by Malcolm Tait and Olive Tayler

The Cyclist's Companion
by George Theohari

The Curry Companion
by Sonja Patel

The Fishing Companion
by Lesley Crawford

The Gardener's Companion
by Vicky Bamforth

The Ideas Companion
by Johnny Acton

The Irish Companion
by Brendan Nolan

The Literary Companion
by Emma Jones

The London Companion
by Jo Swinnerton

The Moviegoer's Companion
by Rhiannon Guy

The Politics Companion
Edited by Daisy Sampson

The Sailing Companion
by Miles Kendall

The Scout's Companion
By Sonja Patel

The Shakespeare Companion
by Emma Jones and Rhiannon Guy

The Stonehenge Companion
by James McClintock

The Traveller's Companion
by Georgina Newbery and Rhiannon Guy

The Walker's Companion
by Malcolm Tait

The Wildlife Companion
by Malcolm Tait and Olive Tayler

SERIES EDITORS

Malcolm Tait, Emma Jones, Jo Swinnerton and Rhiannon Guy

I will honour Christmas in my heart, and try to keep it all the year.

Charles Dickens

First published in Great Britain by Think Books in 2008
This edition published in 2008 by Think Books,
an imprint of Pan Macmillan Ltd
Pan Macmillan, 20 New Wharf Road, London N1 9RR,
Basingstoke and Oxford
Associated companies throughout the world
www.panmacmillan.com
www.think-books.com

ISBN: 978-1-84525-064-5

Author: Sonja Patel
Editor: Jo Swinnerton
Think Books: Tania Adams, James Collins, Rica Dearman,
Camilla Doodson and Marion Thompson

1 3 5 7 9 8 6 4 2

A CIP catalogue record for this book is available from the British Library.

Printed and bound in the UK by CPI Mackays, Chatham

Cover image: Dom Scott

Aren't we forgetting the true meaning of Christmas? You know, the birth of Santa.
Bart Simpson

THANKS

A Merry Christmas, a Splendid Saturnalia, a Lovely Yule and Much Festive Thanks to:

Tom Ellis for putting up with Christmas in July, and all the trimmings

Friends and family, always at the ready with a Christmas cocktail, a bit of tinsel and a toast

The British Library for help with research and the loan of books

Santa, for his constant support (in exchange for...)

INTRODUCTION

'At Christmas play and make good cheer, for Christmas comes but once a year' said 16th-century farmer and author, Thomas Tusser. Today 'once a year' begins in August, when shops start stocking tinsel and a 150-day countdown is the norm.

This kind of excess anticipation could drive many people to veto Christmas altogether, but *The Christmas Companion* argues otherwise, for it shows that Christmas hasn't always come easy. Go back a few thousand years and the etymological definition of Christmas required that a child be born of a virgin, who be known as Christ. Oliver Cromwell and his not so merry Puritans banned Christmas altogether between 1647 and 1660 and it didn't even earn its accepted position on 25 December until 1752, when the entire Christian calendar changed in line with the Pagan winter solstice.

To veto Christmas would not only negate the thousands of years it has taken to amalgamate Pagan and Christian traditions, but also the hard work of our Victorian ancestors: celebrators of the Christmas tree and proud 'parents' of some of Christmas's biggest purveyors – Charles Dickens, Clement Clarke Moore and Mrs Isabella Beeton. For what else can conjure up the spirit of Christmas better than *A Christmas Carol*? Where would we be without those trusted recipes for turkey and mince pies? Indeed, why would we even bother decorating our trees if Victoria and Albert hadn't made such a fuss of theirs? And then there are the Christmas namesakes: take away Christmas and you displace a whole range of mountains, several islands and their mass migrating crabs.

To do away with Christmas would be a shame, for all of the above and not least for the loss of a well-deserved holiday after a hard year's work. But perhaps we should make more of Tusser's advice and make Christmas less about money and more about Christ's birth or 'play and good cheer'. And if you're stuck for inspiration, from what to cook to how to re-enact the World War I Christmas Truce or explain where Santa comes from, just delve into these pages. If nothing else, it might take the edge off Boxing Day.

Sonja Patel, author, *The Christmas Companion*

QUOTE UNQUOTE

Santa Claus is preferable to God in every way but one:
There is no such thing as Santa Claus.
PJ O'Rourke, US political satirist

WHAT IS THE NATIVITY?

Most people know.that the Nativity is the story of the birth of Jesus, accepted by Christians to be the birth of Christ. But where does the story come from?

The Nativity is the story of the birth of Jesus as told in the Gospels and various apocryphal accounts (*apocrypha* from the Greek word for 'hidden'). The Gospels (the word 'Gospel' taken from the Old English for 'good news') are the four canonical books of the New Testament that describe the birth, life, ministry, crucifixion and resurrection of Jesus. These books, written according to St Matthew, St Mark, St Luke and St John, were written between AD65-100. Biblical apocrypha are texts that are often printed as part of the Bible despite their perceived status of being outside of the biblical canon. They are typically printed in a third section apart from the Old and New Testaments. A Biblical canon is a list or set of Biblical books considered to be authoritative as scripture by a particular religious community, generally in Judaism or Christianity. Believers consider these canonical books to be inspired by God or to express the authoritative history of the relationship between God and his people.

It is important to explain that there are various accounts of the Nativity as they can offer conflicting reports, and some people accept various accounts and details while others do not. In terms of the canonical Bible, there are only two accounts of the Nativity and these are in the Gospel of Matthew and the Gospel of Luke. These birth narratives have some elements in common. Both relate that Jesus of Nazareth was the child of Mary, who at the time of his conception was betrothed as the wife of Joseph, said to be a descendant of the Biblical King David. In the Gospel of Luke, Jesus' conception, preceded by an angelic annunciation is presented as miraculous in that he is conceived by the power of the Holy Spirit. In the Gospel of St Matthew, his birth is presented as the fulfilment of prophecies made by the Prophets of Israel. Either way, and again with embellishment from apocryphal texts, the remembrance and re-enactment of the Nativity scene are central to the Christian celebration of Christmas.

...AND A HAPPY NEW YEAR

How the traditional English greeting of 'A Merry Christmas and a Happy New Year' appears around the world...

Basque	*Gabon Zoriontsuak eta urte berri on*
Catalan	*Bon Nadal i Feliç Any Nou*
Danish	*God jul og godt nytår*
Dutch	*Prettige kerstdagen en een gelukkig nieuwjaar*
Estonian	*Häid jõule ja Head uut aastat*
Finnish	*Hyvää Joulua ja Onnellista Uutta Vuotta*
French	*Joyeux Noël et Bonne Année*
German	*Fröhliche Weihnachten und ein glückliches Neues Jahr*
Irish	*Nollaig Shona Duit*
Italian	*Buon Natale e Felice Anno Nuovo*
Polish	*Wesolych Swiat i Szczesliwego Nowego Roku*
Portuguese	*Boas Festas e um feliz Ano novo*
Spanish	*Feliz Navidad y Próspero Año Nuevo*
Swedish	*God Jul och Gott Nytt År*

CHRISTMAS TOWN

Christmas Island, also known as Kiritimati, in the Pacific Ocean has four inhabited towns and one abandoned town. They are:

Banana (Banana Wells)
London
Paris (in ruins)
Poland
Tabwakea

DUMB CAKE, DIVINE

If you're looking for love at Christmastime, then get thee to a kitchen at midnight on Christmas Eve. There you should bake a cake of water, eggs and salt with other bachelors and spinsters and prick your initials into the top of the cake. All this must be done in absolute silence, mind. Then place your cake on the hearthstone and if silence is maintained, then a spirit will prick the initials of your future spouse into the cake alongside yours. If after that you walk backwards to bed, you will dream of your future spouse, too. If all this be true, then it does not deserve its title of dumb cake, but rather a cake that divines, and nor shall you need to make one again.

CHRISTMAS DINNER IN... EASTERN EUROPE

On Christmas Day in Eastern Europe you could be tucking into:

- Twelve meatless dishes (common in Poland, Ukraine and Lithuania)
- Fried carp and potato salad (Czech Republic)
- Christmas biscuits
- *Opłatek* (a large wafer biscuit with a picture of Mary, Joseph and Jesus on it – passed around dinner tables in Poland)

CHRISTMAS CRACKERS

The ones you wish you'd never pulled...

JOKE: What do you have in December that you don't have in any other month?

Answer on page 153

HAPPY SATURNALIA!

One of the major precursors to the Christian celebration of Christmas was the ancient Roman feast of Saturnalia. Dedicated to the Italian deity Saturnus – teacher of the arts of agriculture and god of Nature – this great celebration also brought together two other Roman holidays, Brumelia and Juvenalia. According to *1001 Christmas Facts and Fancies* by Alfred Carl Hottes, published in 1937, Saturnalia lasted from 17-24 December, followed by Calends – a New Year festival – on 1 January. Both were given to days of revelry with processions, eating, drinking, singing, lighting candles, laurel decorations, present giving, the men dressed as women or masqueraded in the hides of animals and the rich and poor equal with no distinction between man and slave. While celebrations could start as harmless fun, many did descend into wild joy and unrestrained orgies of a salacious nature. The emperors also used the feast to their own gains with the senate expected to present New Year's gifts to them. Hottes goes on to describe how Augustus even 'had a nocturnal vision requiring that the people annually present money to him' while in Caligula's case 'he appeared on the porch of his palace on the Calends of January and received gifts of all descriptions'. Both in honour of Saturnus of course, just as many celebrate the birth of Christ with gifts today.

TALES OF CHRISTMAS PAST

From Stave 3: 'The Second of the Three Spirits'

The moment Scrooge's hand was on the lock, a strange voice called him by his name, and bade him enter. He obeyed.

It was his own room. There was no doubt about that. But it had undergone a surprising transformation. The walls and ceiling were so hung with living green, that it looked a perfect grove; from every part of which, bright gleaming berries glistened. The crisp leaves of holly, mistletoe, and ivy reflected back the light, as if so many little mirrors had been scattered there; and such a mighty blaze went roaring up the chimney, as that dull petrifaction of a hearth had never known in Scrooge's time, or Marley's, or for many and many a winter season gone. Heaped up on the floor, to form a kind of throne, were turkeys, geese, game, poultry, brawn, great joints of meat, sucking-pigs, long wreaths of sausages, mince-pies, plum-puddings, barrels of oysters, red-hot chestnuts, cherry-cheeked apples, juicy oranges, luscious pears, immense twelfth-cakes, and seething bowls of punch, that made the chamber dim with their delicious steam. In easy state upon this couch, there sat a jolly Giant, glorious to see, who bore a glowing torch, in shape not unlike Plenty's horn, and held it up, high up, to shed its light on Scrooge, as he came peeping round the door.

"Come in!" exclaimed the Ghost. "Come in, and know me better, man."

Scrooge entered timidly, and hung his head before this Spirit. He was not the dogged Scrooge he had been; and though its eyes were clear and kind, he did not like to meet them.

"I am the Ghost of Christmas Present," said the Spirit. "Look upon me!"

Charles Dickens,
***A Christmas Carol*, 1843**

FESTIVE FLORA AND FAUNA: EVERGREEN

Bringing evergreens into the home around Christmastime is no new thing. Pre-Christian pagans brought branches of holly and ivy into the home to protect and give shelter to the nature spirits that inhabited them. When the first buds started to appear outside, they would 'release' the evergreen spirits in celebration of spring. This tradition continued well into the Middle Ages and was adopted by Christians as a way of merging old beliefs with new. Both St Gregory and St Augustine – founder of the first church in Britain – encouraged their new converts to decorate their homes with leaves, but for the festival of Christ rather than Saturn.

Number of ingredients traditionally used to make a Christmas pudding, 13
allegedly representing Jesus and his disciples

DECK THE HALLS

The tradition for ornamenting our homes with sparkling lights, glass baubles and tinsel stems back several millennia. Here's how some of our favourite modern decorations are said to have come into being...

Baubles: The first type of bauble was made of glass in the 16th century in a place called Lauscha on the Bohemian border area of Germany. Glassblowing was a big industry there and at the end of the day, the glassblowers would drink a lot of ale, and frivolous games would follow. One of these games was to see who could blow the biggest glass ball before it exploded. The baubles that didn't end up in smithereens would be coated on the inside with silver nitrate and taken by the women to market. They were then bought to hang in hallways to ward off evil spirits and adopted as Christmas decorations. When Queen Victoria brought the Christmas tree tradition from Prince Albert's homeland, Germany, the glass baubles from Lauscha came too.

Tinsel: Tinsel was 'invented' in Nuernberg, Germany, in 1610, and originally made of shredded silver. In later years it also contained lead to help it hang better. The fringing effect may well stem from as far back as the peoples of Old Mesopotamia, where great store was placed on fringes – on clothes and on bushes as a symbol of status. The word 'tinsel' may come from the old French word *estincele*, which means 'sparkle'. Although today's tinsel still looks metallic, it is usually made of coated plastic.

Fairy lights: The precursor for fairy lights was the candle. Wax ornaments evolved in Germany, when the honeycombs that imported honey for gingerbread were pushed into the bread-making moulds and sold alongside sweets at market. The first electric lights were produced and displayed by Edward H Johnson, an associate of inventor Thomas Edison, and vice-president of the Edison Electric Light Company in the US. His Christmas-tree lights were hand-wired with 80 red, white and blue incandescent light bulbs the size of walnuts and proudly illuminated on 22 December 1882 at his home in New York.

Candy canes: A straight, white version of the candy cane has been attributed to a French priest in the early 1400s and then bent into a cane shape by a choirmaster at Cologne Cathedral in Germany – or so legend goes. His idea was to bend the straight cane to make it represent a shepherd's staff. Another theory is that candy canes became hooked as a functional solution that allowed them to be hung on trees. The striped version is sometimes attributed to a Protestant candy-maker in the 1870s. He is said to have formed a 'J' for Jesus, made it white to represent his purity, and added three red stripes to stand for the Holy Trinity.

 Number of recorded Christmas Day births in Oxfordshire in 2005

CHRISTMAS IN PICTURES

As he struggled once more with the road map, Santa wished someone would hurry up and invent sat nav.

CHRISTMAS PANTOS: A RECIPE FOR SUCCESS

Key ingredients for a successful Christmas panto:

A traditional storyline
A couple of songs
Much dancing
Obligatory buffoonery
A spoonful of slapstick
Just enough in-jokes
Some audience participation
As many C-class celebrities as you can muster
A spattering of sexual innuendo (designed to go over the heads of small children)

Number of Christmas shows used to collect great moments for A Bing Crosby Christmas *– a DVD released in 1998* 15

NATIVITY TRADITIONS OF THE WORLD: PROVENCE, FRANCE

The Nativity scene is beloved by Christians around the world, with many cultures and customs 'making it their own'...

Nativity scenes in Provence are sometimes composed of hundreds of small clay figurines, called santons. These are designed to represent all the traditional trades and professions of old Provence. They are often collected as art or craft objects, even by non-believers of the Nativity.

ON THAT CHRISTMAS DAY

Historic events that took place on Christmas Day...

1914 The Christmas Truce of World War I: German and British troops temporarily cease fire

1932 A magnitude 7.6 earthquake hits Gansu, China, killing 70,000 people

1941 The Japanese occupation of Hong Kong begins

1947 The Constitution of the Republic of China goes into effect

1950 The 'Stone of Scone' is stolen from Westminster Abbey by Scottish nationalists; it later turns up on 11 April 1951

1974 Messiah wannabe Marshall Fields drives a vehicle through the gates of the White House, resulting in a four-hour standoff

1979 The Soviet Union airlifts forces into Afghanistan to begin its occupation

1989 Nicolae Ceausescu and his wife Elena are condemned to death under a range of charges relating to their dictatorship in Romania

1990 The first successful trial of the system that would become the World Wide Web takes place

1991 Mikhail Gorbachev resigns as president of the Soviet Union

2003 The Beagle 2 probe, released from the *Mars Express* spacecraft on 19 December, disappears shortly before its scheduled landing

2004 The *Cassini* orbiter releases Huygens probe, which successfully lands on Saturn's moon Titan, on 14 January 2005

 Century in which the turkey was first introduced to England, gaining its name from a mix-up with another import, the Turkish guinea fowl

'THE NAME'S CHRISTMAS'

If your surname is Christmas, then you may have been interested in a report by the BBC in December 2005. It told of a team of scientists in Oxford who were trying to prove whether families with the rare surname Christmas all descended from a single male ancestor. The work was part of wider research that was looking at the links between surnames and DNA, and aimed to look at similarities or differences in the male, or Y, chromosomes of volunteers. At the time, researchers were appealing for Christmas volunteers. However, they were already being assisted by one Henry Christmas, a former telecommunications engineer who had spent 50 years researching the origins and history of his surname. His research shows that the Christmas family name is established widely through the Home Counties, with two significant clusters in Essex and Sussex. Henry also disagrees with one genealogical explanation of where the surname Christmas comes from – that which denotes it stems from those who were born at Christmas. According to Henry, the original spelling of the name was Chrystmasse, which perhaps indicates a Norman origin. He has also found that some Huguenots came over from France with that name. What remains to be seen is if any of the Christmases are related to Father Christmas himself...

QUOTE UNQUOTE

A goose never voted for an early Christmas.
Irish saying

TALES OF CHRISTMAS PAST

Eight of us set out that night. There was Sixpence the Tanner, who had never sung in his life (he just worked his mouth in church); the brothers Horace and Boney, who were always fighting everybody and always getting the worst of it; Clergy Green, the preaching maniac; Walt the bully, and my two brothers. As we went down the lane other boys, from other villages, were already about the hills, bawling 'Kingwenslush', and shouting through keyholes 'Knock on the knocker! Ring the Bell! Give us a penny for singing so well!' They weren't an approved charity, as we were, the Choir; but competition was in the air.

Laurie Lee (1914-1997), *Cider with Rosie*, 1959

CELEBRITY CHRISTMAS TREES

Just some of the biggest and brightest Christmas trees in the world:

- Rich's Great Tree, Atlanta
- Rockefeller Center Christmas Tree, New York
- Victoria Square, Adelaide
- The National Enquirer Building, Lantana, Florida (no longer erected)
- White House Lawn, Washington, DC

THE MUPPET CHRISTMAS CAROL... IN 60 SECONDS

A brief synopsis of the 1992 film The Muppet Christmas Carol, *so that you can get your fix of Muppet mayhem at any time of year...*

Muppet and Christmas fans were overjoyed when Jim Henson's son Brian and his team decided to bring out this feature-length musical adaptation of Charles Dickens' *A Christmas Carol*. The team also scored a major coup by getting Michael Caine to star as Ebenezer Scrooge. This version is narrated by the Great Gonzo as Dickens (with occasional commentary by Rizzo the Rat), and tells the story of Scrooge (Caine), a miserly moneylender who is more interested in profit than celebration. Kermit the Frog plays the part of Bob Cratchit, who has to beg Scrooge to let him have Christmas Day off work. Scrooge is then visited by his nephew who asks him to Christmas dinner, and by some gentlemen who come to collect money for the poor. He rebuffs them both and is then visited by the apparitions of his former business partners, Jacob and Robert Marley, who have been condemned to shackles in the afterlife for their miserly actions on Earth. They warn Scrooge of further visitations by the spirits of Christmas. That night, Scrooge is visited by: the Ghost of Christmas Past who shows him his former employer Mr Fozziwig, played by Fozzie Bear; the Ghost of Christmas Present; and the Ghost of Christmas Yet to Come. The final ghost tells Scrooge that Tiny Tim, played by Robin the Frog, will not survive the coming year because the Cratchit family is so poor. Scrooge is prompted to see the error of his ways and ends up planning a feast for Bob Cratchit, Tiny Tim and the rest of the family, including the veritable Miss Piggy as Mrs Cratchit. Scrooge also learns to adopt the spirit of Christmas throughout the year.

 Date in December in the Julian calendar on which the Romans celebrated the second day of Saturnalia, a winter feast

BEST-SELLING ALBUMS OF CHRISTMAS PAST – 1950s

From the British Library's *Pop Goes the Library* exhibition in association with The Official UK Charts Company, 26 July 2006 to 25 March 2007. More than 20% of albums are sold in December alone, many ending up in Christmas stockings.

1956	*The King and I*	Original Soundtrack
1957	*The King and I*	Original Soundtrack
1958	*South Pacific*	Original Soundtrack
1959	*South Pacific*	Original Soundtrack

STEVEN THE RED-NOSED REINDEER?

An alternative list of flying reindeers were used in the *South Park* 'Christmas Special Red Sleigh Down'. The traditional reindeer had to be replaced because they were shot down when Santa tried to take Christmas to Iraq. Fortunately Santa was then saved by:

Chantel • Fluffy • Horace
Montel • Patches • Rainbow
Skippy • Steven

IF YOU WERE A CHRISTMAS ISLAND CRAB...

...you would be a red-coloured species of terrestrial crab, endemic to Christmas Island and the Cocos Islands in the Indian Ocean. Although restricted to a relatively small area you would have 120 million friends and family. You would live on a diet of mostly fallen leaves and flowers, although sometimes you might snack on other animals, including red crabs, making you a part-time cannibal. You would live in a burrow, in order to shelter from the sun, since you still breathe through gills and the possibility of dying out is a great danger for you. But, mostly, you would be among the most celebrated of all crabs, for your annual migration to the sea in order to lay your eggs in the ocean. You cover your routes to the coast so densely that you can be seen from the air, making you famous by land, air and sea. You don't celebrate Christmas. Christmas celebrates you.

Century in which Christmas trees were first introduced to England, under the rule of Queen Victoria and inspired by her consort, Prince Albert 19

TALES OF CHRISTMAS PAST

Christmas Day

We had not been long home when the sound of music was heard from a distance. A band of country lads, without coats, their shirt sleeves fancifully tied with ribbons, their hats decorated with greens, and clubs in their hands, was seen advancing up the avenue, followed by a large number of villagers and peasantry. They stopped before the hall-door, where the music struck up a peculiar air, and the lads performed a curious and intricate dance, advancing, retreating and striking their clubs together, keeping exact time to the music; while one, whimsically crowned with a fox's skin, the tail of which flaunted down his back, kept capering round the skirts of the dance, and rattling a Christmas box with many antic gesticulations.

The squire eyed this fanciful exhibition with great interest and delight, and gave me a full account of its origin, which he traced to the times when the Romans held possession of the island; plainly proving that this was a lineal descendant of the sword dance of the ancients. "It was now," he said, "nearly extinct, but he had accidentally met with traces of it in the neighbourhood and had encouraged its revival; though, to tell the truth, it was too apt to be followed up by the rough cudgel play, and broken heads in the evening."

Washington Irving, *Old Christmas: from the sketch-book of Washington Irving*, 1886

QUOTE UNQUOTE

Christmas won't be Christmas without any presents.
Jo March in the opening lines of *Little Women*
by Louisa May Alcott

BRZEZINSKI'S MUPPET CHRISTMAS

In 1978, the Muppets joined Carter Administration National Security Advisor Zbigniew Brzezinski for an evening of fun, song and anti-communist rhetoric. What they got was a duet of 'Winter Wonderland' with Miss Piggy and an incongruous and eyebrow-raising scene with Brzezinski dressing as an Afghan mujahideen and explaining the true meaning of Christmas to an assemblage of Muppets. Washington rumour, albeit unsupported by any Carter administration member, had it that the President had the special on a loop while he drafted his infamous 'Malaise' speech.

20 *Date in November 2007 on which the Regent Street Christmas tree lights were officially switched on by the shoppers themselves*

CHRISTMAS CRACKERS

The ones you wish you'd never pulled...

JOKE: What do elves learn in school?

Answer on page 153

PANTO PARTS

Some of the major recurring characters in a Christmas pantomime and who should play them:

The principal boy – Beautiful young actress with good legs
The pantomime dame – Ugly actor in drag; can be oversized
The animal (cow or horse) – Two actors and a four-legged suit
The good fairy – Good-looking actress; preferably over 40
The villain – Actor with an interesting face
The fool – Self-declared comedy genius

SANTA'S LITTLE HELPERS: JULTOMEN AND JULBOCK

Luckily for Santa, delivering all the presents at Christmas isn't just up to him and his tribe of elves and reindeer – a whole troop of gift-givers are out and about spreading their joy. As long as you've been a good little girl or boy that is...

In Sweden, Jultomen, translated as 'The Yule Man', traditionally brings Christmas gifts. Like the Danish and Norwegian Julnisse and Nisse, Jultomen is a small gnome who is said to bring protection and good luck to the home and its inhabitants. He is said to live in the barn and is noted for his long white beard. If you leave a bowl of porridge or rice pudding for him, he will deliver presents for the children and bring good luck to the home for the following year. Some say he also travels by sleigh drawn by the Julbock or the Yule Goat, although this figure stands on its own as a Christmas figurehead in Sweden. Although it became customary for men of the villages to dress up as the Julbock and play pranks on the unsuspecting, he is most often seen in homes around the country as a Christmas ornament made of straw or roughly hewn wood. His origins may go back to Norse mythology when the God of Thunder, Thor – in whose honour Yule logs were first lit in winter – was said to ride through the sky in a chariot drawn by two goats, Tanngrisnir and Tanngnjóstr. Not unlike Santa Claus...

The first of two dates in December that the winter solstice, or the ancient interpretation of Yule, occurs in the Northern Hemisphere

OH CHRISTMAS TREE, OH CHRISTMAS TREE

The Christmas tree symbolises much that Christmas has become: a canvas for our favourite decorations and religious attire, a celebration of nature with which to adorn our homes and, of course, shade for our growing piles of presents. So where did the custom come from?

Tradition credits St Boniface with the species of tree that we place at the centre of our celebrations. In a stage-managed confrontation with old gods and local heathen tribes, Boniface was said to have chopped down the Oak of Thor at Geismar – a Patron tree that held particular significance for ancient pagan Germanic tribes – and a fir then grew in its place. He laid claim to the tree as a new symbol of life with which to build homes and bring Christ into the centre of them, the evergreen leaves representing constant light.

The modern custom of erecting and decorating a Christmas tree can be traced back to the 16th century. Records of the Cathedral of Strasbourg mention the erection of a Christmas tree in 1539, while later guilds are recorded to have placed Christmas trees in front of their guildhalls. They would be decorated with apples, nuts, dates, pretzels and paper flowers and the children would then collect the offerings on Christmas Day.

The custom spread through mainly Protestant towns on the upper Rhineland. It then infiltrated the largely Catholic population of the lower Rhine through Prussian officials who settled there in 1815. Around this time, the custom also became popular among European nobility, spread as far as Russia; Princess Henrietta of Nassau-Weilburg had one in Vienna in 1816 and the Duchesse d'Orléans followed suit with one in 1840.

In Britain, the Christmas tree tradition was introduced by George III's Queen Charlotte of Mecklenburg-Strelitz but stayed largely within the royal family. Queen Victoria was particularly enchanted with the custom, and after her marriage to the German Prince Albert, it became more widespread. A picture of Victoria and Albert and family with their tree was published in the *London Illustrated News* in December 1848 and like other royal traditions, later copied in America. The trend was now truly transatlantic, although many US towns with Germanic connections still battle it out in the 'first ever' Christmas tree wars.

Today, over 36 million Christmas trees are produced in the US and around 60 million in Europe. Even as plastic trees gain popularity with those needled by the real thing, it doesn't look as if the tradition will die out any time soon.

22 *The second and most common date in December that the winter solstice, or the ancient interpretation of Yule, occurs in the Northern Hemisphere*

CHRISTMAS IN PICTURES

Arabella couldn't get enough of
Lucy's Christmas pudding.

CHRISTMAS DINNER IN... MEXICO

On Christmas Day in Mexico you could be tucking into:

- Fruits (oranges, limes and other tropical fruits)
- Salad (including jimica, beets, bananas and peanuts)
- Pozole (stew made of pork or beef and hominy in red chili sauce)
- Menudo (stew of beef tripe and hominy in red chili sauce)
- Tamales (filled steam-cooked sour dough served with cream and crumbly cheese)
- Atole with buñuelos (thinned hot chocolate pudding with fried flour tortillas, sugar and cinnamon)
- Sweet tamales (corn with raisins, sweet beans or strawberry flavoured)

THE ART OF THE ORNAMENT

Every year since 1988 The Tate has commissioned a leading contemporary artist to design its Christmas Tree. It is then exhibited in the Rotunda – the glass-domed hall and gallery of the Tate Britain. Twenty years on we can compare the trees across three decades, many symbolising issues that were important at the time.

1989 Tim Head

Head produced a Christmas tree installation taking the motif for the tree shapes from a symbol printed on the packaging of a commercial cleaning product. The synthetic nature of these decorations contrasted with the real tree, although a dead magpie perched on top of it reminded the viewer that the tree was dead too. The work was designed to comment on the ecological implications of the consumer society in which we live.

1999 Mat Collishaw

Collishaw presented a traditionally decorated Christmas tree, complete with angel at the top and presents around the base – but with a twist: at the foot of the tree there also lay a video of rats running around and nibbling mince pies in their own festive celebration. The rats were designed to remind the viewer of what lies beneath the surface glitter of Christmas.

See the Christmas trees at
www.tate.org.uk/britain/exhibitions/christmastree

QUOTE UNQUOTE

The one thing women don't want to find in their stockings on Christmas morning is their husband.
Joan Rivers, US comedian

GIVE ME SOME DOUGH

This Christmas, instead of asking for cashback at the supermarket, why not ask your baker for some 'Yule dough'. In the *Westminster Review* in 1905, this was described as 'a flat cake in the shape of a baby, which bakers presented to their customers in the same manner that chandlers presented Christmas candles'. If you don't get your dough then reprimand your baker for not partaking in the Yule spirit and urge him or her to bring back the tradition next year.

24 *Date in December of Christmas Eve, and the date in 1777 that James Cook discovered Kiritimati, one of the world's Christmas Islands*

LOOK BEHIND YOU!

And other ways to take part in the Christmas panto:

'Look behind you!'
'Oh yes it is!'
'On no it isn't!'
'Boo!'
'Awwww'

CHRISTMAS TRUCE TRUTHS

The Christmas Truce is a much-written about event, that took place during World War I between German and British or French troops in 1914. However, there are many myths that exist. In a 'Frequently asked questions' article, the dedicated website www.christmastruce.co.uk and its Operation Plum Pudding campaign – put together through memories and letters by those involved or those close to them – attempt to find the truth:

Did it really happen?
Yes. The many letters from soldiers who took part are more than sufficient evidence. Many of these letters were published in the soldiers' local paper – usually sent in to the paper by astonished families. Operation Plum Pudding aims to republish these letters in a single source.

How widespread was the truce?
It's difficult to be exact at the moment but certainly hundreds of soldiers took part. However, on some parts of the Western Front there was no truce and fighting continued as normal.

How long did it last?
In many cases just two or three days. In other cases until New Year's Day. There is some evidence a truce of sorts existed until March (and was rekindled at Easter). But no truce occurred during any other Christmas in World War I.

What was the official response?
Fury! Once the letters were published in newspapers (censorship was in its infancy) the top brass demanded names – but no action was ever taken against participants.

Did the Germans really win 3-2 in the football match?
There's still some doubt over whether the match took place. Hopefully Operation Plum Pudding will answer this question once and for all. If our researchers can find first-hand accounts by those who watched or took part in the match it should be sufficient evidence. Readers are encouraged to write in to the website with their evidence...

DREAMING OF A GREEN CHRISTMAS?

Every day there are reports about the environment and how you can do your bit to help protect it. Christmas is no exception, and there are plenty of things you can do to be more eco-friendly. You could also save up to £8 million of electricity each year. There are some top tips from the Energy Saving Trust at www.energysavingtrust.co.uk.

- Switch from conventional to LED Christmas lights to reduce your energy consumption by 90% – because they don't generate as much heat you could also be making your tree safer
- Save energy by turning one or more room lights off when you switch on your Christmas tree lights – it makes the illuminated tree look more attractive too
- When buying gifts, choose products with minimal packaging
- To cut down on waste, wrap presents in recycled paper from gifts you receive – use ribbon or string to wrap presents so it's easier for your paper to be reused too
- Look for cards made from recycled paper – or send e-cards instead
- Give unwanted presents to a good home or charity
- Don't forget to take reusable bags with you when you are Christmas shopping

IF YOU WERE A CHRISTMAS TREE WORM...

...you would also go by the name *Spirobranchus giganteus* and be described as a tube-dwelling worm. Your comparison to a Christmas tree would stem from your colourful plumes – two each, in total – made up of feathery gills. You would live on a coral reef and draw back into your tube when alarmed. Which is a shame as you are such a gay creature, in shades of beautiful orange, blue and pink as well as many other colours. Of course, your 'feathers' are not just for decoration. You use them to filter tiny plankton out of the water column to eat and to breathe. Just like a Christmas tree uses its pine needles to get the energy it needs and to breathe in carbon dioxide and breathe out oxygen. You also come in male and female form, having separate sexes that reproduce by casting eggs and sperm into the water. Once fertilised, the eggs develop into tiny larvae that settle on coral heads and burrow in to grow. You do this very well and are thankfully not a threatened species. Which is good, because your presence means the fish and other marine life get a Christmas tree too, and for them the joy is all year round.

26 *Date in December of Boxing Day, a public holiday in the UK, Canada, New Zealand, Australia and many other Commonwealth nations*

KNOW YOUR LIMITS

Festive celebrations can often lead to one tipple too many, which is not always good for your liver. If you know you're going to be doing some extra socialising, remember government guidelines recommend that women should drink no more than 2-3 units of alcohol per day and men should drink no more than 3-4 units per day to avoid damaging their health. Alcohol Concern has a rough guide for what you're drinking, to see how you measure up. Follow it to try and get through Christmas with your health intact:

A pint of normal-strength beer .... *2 units*
A 25ml measure of spirits .... *1 unit*
A 175ml glass of wine (12%) .... *2 units*
A 250ml glass of wine (12%) .... *3 units*
A 330ml alcopop (4.5-5.5%) .... *2 units*
A 440ml can of strong lager (4.6-6%) .... *3 units*

BEST-SELLING ALBUMS OF CHRISTMAS PAST – 1960s

From the British Library's *Pop Goes the Library* exhibition in association with The Official UK Charts Company, 26 July 2006 to 25 March 2007. More than 20% of albums are sold in December alone, many ending up in Christmas stockings.

1960	*South Pacific*	Original Soundtrack
1961	*Another Black and White Minstrel Show*	George Mitchell Minstrels
1962	*The Black and White Minstrel Show*	George Mitchell Minstrels
1963	*With the Beatles*	The Beatles
1964	*Beatles for Sale*	The Beatles
1965	*Rubber Soul*	The Beatles
1966	*The Sound of Music*	Original Soundtrack
1967	*Sergeant Pepper's Lonely Hearts Club Band*	The Beatles
1968	*The Beatles*	The Beatles
1969	*Abbey Road*	The Beatles

Date in December 1831 on which Charles Darwin began his scientific exploration aboard the HMS Beagle, *spending four Christmases 'at sea'*

QUOTE UNQUOTE

Both sides advanced further during one Christmas piss-up than they did in the next two-and-a-half years of war.

Captain Blackadder in the final episode of *Blackadder Goes Forth*, feeling sore after being ruled offside during a football game with the Germans in a reminiscence of the 1914 Christmas Truce

TALES OF CHRISTMAS PAST

I have been looking on, this evening, at a merry company of children assembled round that pretty German toy, a Christmas-Tree. The tree was planted in the middle of the great round table, and towered high above their heads. It was brilliantly lighted by a multitude of little tapers; and everywhere sparkled and glittered with bright objects. There were rosy-cheeked dolls, hiding behind the green leaves; there were real watches (with moveable hands, at least, and an endless capacity of being wound up) dangling from innumerable twigs; there were French polished tables, chairs, bedsteads, wardrobes, eight-day clocks, and various other articles of domestic furniture (wonderfully made, in tin, at Wolverhampton), perched among the boughs, as if in preparation for some fairy house-keeping; there were jolly, broad-faced little men, much more agreeable in appearance than many real men – and no wonder, for their heads took off, and showed them to be full of sugar-plums; there were fiddles and drums; there were tambourines, books, work-boxes, paint-boxes, sweetmeat boxes, peep-show boxes, all kinds of boxes, there were trinkets for the elder girls, far brighter than any grown-up gold and jewels; there were baskets and pincushions in all devices, there were guns, swords, and banners; there were witches standing in enchanted rings of pasteboard, to tell fortunes; there were teetotums, humming-tops, needle-cases, pen-wipers, smelling bottles, conversation cards, bouquet-holders, real fruit, made artificially dazzling with gold leaf; imitation apples, pears and walnuts, crammed with surprises; in short as a pretty child, before me, delightedly whispered to another pretty child, her bosom friend, "There was everything, and more."

Charles Dickens, *A Christmas Tree*, a story published in a compilation of Christmas tales entitled *Christmas Books*, 1861. (The books were printed in two volumes and also contained *A Christmas Carol*, *The Chimes*, *The Cricket on the Hearth*, *The Battle of Life* and *The Haunted Man*.)

A FURRY, FIERY CHRISTMAS

For one family in February 2007, Christmas was nearly over, more than 10 months before it was due – Christmas their pet hamster, that is. Furry friend to the Bell family, Christmas was moved into the kitchen one night because he was keeping their four-year-old son Dylan awake. Unfortunately for Christmas, his cage was left on top of an oven and the hob was turned on by mistake. The cage burst into flames and Christmas became a furry fireball. But, firefighters came to the rescue. When they arrived to put out the blaze, the rodent was on his back with his little charred legs up in the air and his tongue hanging out. Fire officers, including Mark Spinks, gave him a blast of oxygen, a few nips of Ribena and rubbed his belly, and were amazed to see him splutter back to life. One thing the Bell family now know for sure – they'll never take Christmas for granted ever again.

SCENT A CARD

In 2004 the German post office gave away 20 million scented stickers with the aim of making Christmas cards smell even sweeter. Scents included:

Baked apple
Christmas tree (Fir)
Cinnamon
Gingerbread
Honey-wax candle
Orange

FESTIVE FLORA AND FAUNA: THE HOLLY BOUGH

The holly bough took shape in medieval times when two garlands of evergreen – holly, bay, ivy, yew, rosemary and mistletoe – would be combined to make a spherical shape. The garland would also be decorated with ribbons, fruits and gilded nuts, and within the bough a nativity scene placed. The 'holy bough', as it would be called, was hung from a beam near the entrance of the home and visitors encouraged to embrace below it as a symbol of peace and love at Christmastime. Some think the tradition for kissing under mistletoe also stems from this idea, others that the 'holy bough' became 'holly bough' even though other types of leaves can be used.

Date in December 1170 that Thomas Becket was murdered in Canterbury Cathedral, shortly after preaching from there on Christmas Day 29

THE NATIVITY: THE ANGEL GABRIEL

Some things you may or may not know about principal characters in the Nativity:

- Gabriel's first Biblical appearance is as a vision to the prophet Daniel in the Book of Daniel 8:15
- Gabriel is most well known as the angel who serves as a messenger from God to foretell Mary about Jesus' birth
- Christians also believe Gabriel to have foretold the birth of John the Baptist to Zacharias
- Muslims believe Gabriel or Jibril was the medium through which God revealed the Qur'an to Muhammad
- Gabriel is sometimes portrayed in art and literature as androgynous or female
- Gabriel's visit to Joseph to reassure him of Mary's pregnancy is described in the New Testament Gospel of St Matthew 1:18-21
- Gabriel's visit to Mary is often called the Annunciation and is celebrated on 26 March in the Eastern Orthodox and Catholic churches
- The Annunciation is described in the New Testament Gospel of St Luke 1:26-27
- Gabriel, Michael and Satan (the fallen angel) are the only three angels mentioned by name in the canonical Bible
- Only Michael, not Gabriel, is named as an archangel (chief angel) in the canonical Bible; however Gabriel is generally assumed to be an archangel along with Raphael and sometimes Uriel
- The word 'angel' actually comes from the Greek *angelos* meaning 'messenger'
- Although the characteristics of angels are sometimes described in the canonical Bible, the only ones to have wings are of the order cherubim and seraphim
- Some schools of thought consider Gabriel to be of the cherubim order, thereby giving him wings
- Some angel references in the Bible include 'His body was like chrysolite' – chrysolite being a yellow gem stone – and 'clothes were white as snow', from which modern depictions of angels may have evolved
- In the canonical Bible, angels appear most often to humans as ordinary people

 Percentage increase of cans and glass collected over the Christmas period, according to Waste Online in 2007

WARM UP WITH EGGNOG

No 19th-century Christmas soiree would be complete without a bowl of eggnog, a heart-warming sweet cocktail, which, when enough brandy is included, could melt the snow from anyone's nose. Courtesy of www.victoriana.com we find a recipe from *The Whitehouse Cookbook*, published in 1887, that directs drinkers thus:

Beat the yolks of twelve eggs very light, stir in as much white sugar as they will dissolve, pour in gradually one glass of brandy to cook the egg, one glass of old whisky, one grated nutmeg, and three pints of rich milk. Beat the whites to a froth and stir in last.

We add the important instruction: Drink and make merry.

CHRISTMAS CRACKERS

The ones you wish you'd never pulled...

JOKE: Why was Santa's little helper feeling depressed?

Answer on page 153

BORN IN A BUTCHERS?

Bethlehem, where the New Testament says that Christ was born for which we celebrate Christmas, can be translated from the Arabic *Beit Lachem* to mean 'House of Meat' or from the Hebrew *Beit Lehem* to mean 'House of Bread', where *bei* means 'house', *lachem* means 'meat' and *lehem* means 'bread'. However, many scholars think that both names stem from what was once called the 'House of Lahmo', who was the Chaldean god of fertility, worshipped as Lahama by the Canaanites. This ancient tribe are said to have settled there some 3,000 years before the birth of Christ and built a temple to Lahama on the present mount of the Nativity, which overlooks the fertile valleys of the region. Meat, bread or manger, it seems that Jesus was born in very fertile land and Bethlehem continues as one of Palestine's most prosperous areas today. Holy sites that are particularly popular at Christmas include the Church of the Nativity in Manger Square, the Shepherds' Fields, and the Milk Grotto Chapel where Mary supposedly spilled a few drops of breast milk while feeding baby Jesus, turning the cavern milky white.

WHAT'S IN THE BOX?

Boxing Day is usually held on 26 December, the day after Christmas. But what's the 'Box' all about? Here are some common explanations...

- In English tradition, a clay box would be placed in artisan shops for employees and customers to fill with their donations of seasonal goodwill. After Christmas, the box would be shattered and all the contents shared among the workers of the shop. The box was known as the 'Christmas Box' and allowed satisfied masters and customers to bestow a bonus to workers anonymously. The habit of breaking the box on the day after Christmas produced the term 'Boxing Day', while the term 'Christmas Box' can still be used today to denote a seasonal bonus.

- Boxing Day was the day when employers gave a present – known as a box, perhaps by the shape it took – to their staff. Servants were also known to carry boxes to their employers on the day after Christmas, into which coins would be placed. This also formed a precursor to the Christmas bonus.

- In feudal times, Christmas was a reason for gathering large families together. This also applied to serfs and servants who would gather their families in the house of their master or lord. On the day after Christmas the lord was obliged to give each family a box of practical goods such as cloth, grain and tools. For many poverty-stricken serfs this would be the highlight of the year.

- In churches it was traditional to open the donation box on Christmas Day and distribute the money to the less fortunate or lower-class citizens. Some say that the box of Boxing Day refers to this donation box and the act of sharing it.

- On the day after Christmas, the king of the birds – the wren – would be captured and put into a box. The box would then be taken around the village where each household would ask the wren for a successful year and good harvest. Testament to this theory can be found in popular wassailing songs that see characters such as John the Rednose, Milder and Malder hunting a 'cutty wren' and putting it in a box.

- Christmas Day may have been a feast of a holiday for the lord of the manor and his friends. Of course that meant more work for the servants and staff and no special time with their families. As a gesture of goodwill they were generally given the next day off to 'do Christmas'. For many, Christmas dinner comprised a box of leftovers from the master's table, hence the name Boxing Day.

32 *Year in the 20th century that the first Royal Christmas Message was broadcast, by King George V on the BBC Empire Service*

CHRISTMAS IN PICTURES

Lord Melchett's opinion that the turkey was a little overdone did not go down well with Cook.

QUOTE UNQUOTE

Christmas is doing a little something extra for someone.
Charles M Schulz, US cartoonist

HAVE YOURSELF A PUNK ROCK CHRISTMAS

Some alternative Christmas albums and singles from www.mistletunes.com...

(It's Gonna Be a) Punk Rock Christmas	The Ravers	1977
White Christmas	Patti Smith	1978
The Yobs Christmas Album	The Yobs	1980
Santa Claus is Comin' To Town	The Mysteroids	1981
Bollocks to Christmas	Various Artists	1981

The estimated age, in years, of Jesus when he was crucified, calculated by using canonical and apocryphal texts

Several days later, on Christmas Eve, real havoc broke loose. From the balcony of my room at the Sheraton, I could see the entire city. There were powder flashes and staccato bursts in every neighbourhood. Rockets whistled. Huge explosions illuminated the surrounding hills. A dozen blasts came inside the hotel compound itself. Bits of debris flew past my head. The brazen face of war? No, firecrackers.

Everybody in Latin America likes to set off firecrackers on Christmas Eve, but nobody likes it more than the Salvadorans. They have everything – cherry bombs, M80s, defingering little strings of one-inchers and items of ordnance that can turn a fifty-five-gallon oil drum into a steel hula skirt. The largest have a warning printed on them, that they shouldn't be lit by drunks. I am no stranger to loud noise. I've been to a Mitch Ryder and the Detroit Wheels concert. I once dated a woman with two kids. But at midnight on Christmas Eve – with the windows shut, the air-conditioner on, the TV turned up and the bathroom door closed – I couldn't hear myself sing 'Wild Colonial Boy' in the shower. On Christmas Day I saw people raking their yards, gathering mounds of spent gray firecrackers as large as autumn leaf piles.

You'd think after six years of civil war and 464 years of civil unrest, more explosions would be the last thing the Salvadorans would want. Or maybe, the thing they want most.

PJ O'Rourke, from *Christmas in El Salvador*, a story about a Christmas trip to El Salvador, in December 1985 for the book *Holidays from Hell*, 1988

NATIVITY TRADITIONS OF THE WORLD: MEXICO

The Nativity scene is beloved by Christians around the world, with many cultures and customs 'making it their own'...

In Mexico, it is traditional to build the Nativity scene on 16 December, the first day of the *Posada*, meaning 'Inns' and describing a nine-day celebration of the trials Mary and Joseph endured before finding a place to stay. The Nativity is taken from door to door on each evening during the *Posada*, by *peregrinos* or 'pilgrims' – the adults and children of the town or village. The third house they approach will let them in and prayers will be said around the Nativity scene.

 Street number around which the film Miracle on 34th Street *is based, in which a Santa impersonator is declared mad and then defended as real*

TO THE SUN

The winter solstice – a precursor to the festivities of Christmas – might signify the shortest day of the year, but that also means you get the longest night, and days start brightening up over the next six months. Here's when you should celebrate in the years to come:

Year	Date	Time
2008	21	12.04
2009	21	17.47
2010	21	23.38
2011	22	05.30
2012	21	11.11
2013	21	17.11
2014	21	23.03

THE KING'S SPEECH: A MESSAGE TO THE EMPIRE

The first royal recording was made by George V and Queen Mary to mark Empire Day in 1923. The edited transcript below forms part of the first royal Christmas Day broadcast on the radio – also by George V – published as a commercial 78rpm disc and the start of a tradition that continues today.

'Through one of the marvels of modern science, I am enabled, this Christmas Day, to speak to all my peoples throughout the Empire. I take it as a good omen that wireless should have reached its present perfection at a time when the Empire has been linked in closer union, for it offers us immense possibilities to make that union closer still.

'It may be that our future will lay upon us more than one stern test. Our past will have taught us how to meet it unshaken. For the present, the work to which we are all equally bound is to arrive at a reasoned tranquillity within our borders, to regain prosperity without self-seeking and to carry with us those whom the burden of past years has disheartened or overborne. My life's aim has been to serve as I might towards those ends, for your loyalty, your confidence in me, has been my abundant reward.

'I speak now from my home and from my heart to you all. To men and women so cut off by the snows, the deserts or the seas, that only voices out of the air can reach them; to those cut off from fuller life by blindness, sickness or infirmity; and to those who are celebrating this day with their children and their grandchildren; to all, to each, I wish a happy Christmas. God bless you.'

Estimated percentage of UK holidaymakers who took a city break at Christmas, according to a survey by ABTA in 2006 35

CHRISTMAS CRACKERS

The ones you wish you'd never pulled...

JOKE: What's the most popular wine at Christmas?

Answer on page 153

THE MYTH OF THE NATIVITY

Do conflicting accounts of the Nativity render it a myth? Some scholars think so...

Because the canonical Gospels of St Matthew and St Luke present two different accounts of the Nativity, many scholars see these stories either as completely fictional accounts or at least constructed from traditions that predate the Gospels. Some contradictions include the following account details:

St Matthew	St Luke
Angel appears in a dream to Joseph	No mention
Wise men coming from the east	No mention
Massacre of the Innocents by Herod	No mention
Joseph, Mary and Jesus' Flight to Egypt	No mention
No mention	Conception and birth of John the Baptist
No mention	Angel appears to Mary
No mention	World census
No mention	Birth in a manger
No mention	Choir of angels at the birth
Family live in Nazareth	Implication of family living in Bethlehem
Family move to Bethlehem only for census	Family move to Nazareth after Egypt
Dated to Herod the Great (died 4BC)	Dated to Census of Quirinius (AD6)

 Estimated number in millions of Christmas trees produced in the US each year to cope with demand, according to a 2007 report

SANTA'S LITTLE HELPERS: BABUSHKA

Luckily for Santa, delivering all the presents at Christmas isn't just up to him and his tribe of elves and reindeer – a whole troop of gift-givers are out and about spreading their joy. As long as you've been a good little girl or boy that is...

In Russia, a little old woman called Babushka is celebrated at Christmas. Babushka is a diminutive of *baba*, meaning 'old woman', and widely used as 'grandmother' in Russian.

The story goes that Babushka lived in a small Russian village where she was known to have the cleanest house. One day a star appeared over the village but Babushka was too busy to see what all the fuss was about. Then a knock came on her door. To her surprise, there were three Magi – kings from a faraway land. They asked if they could rest there. The Magi told her that they were on a journey to find a newborn king, a King of Earth and Heaven. They showed her gifts of Gold, Frankincense and Myrrh: 'Come with us', they urged. But Babushka didn't have a gift to bring – until she remembered her cupboard full of toys. Sadly her baby son had died and these were all she had left of him. She told the Magi that she would think about joining them. But when the Magi left, she didn't go with them. She had too much cleaning to do, including the toys. Suddenly Babushka panicked: she must find this newborn King. Everywhere she went she said, 'Have you seen the kings?' Finally, someone told her that they had gone to Bethlehem. Sadly when she arrived at the stable where the newborn King was born, everyone had left. The innkeeper told her that the kings had returned home and the Baby Jesus had fled to Egypt with his family. It is said that Babushka is still looking for the newborn King and while she does, delivers her toys to other little children instead.

CELEBRITY PANTOMIMERS

Just some of the celebrities who have taken part in our Christmas pantomimes, some to better effect than others:

Ian McKellen	Widow Twankey	*Aladdin*
Henry Winkler	Captain Hook	*Peter Pan*
Patrick Duffy	Baron Hardup	*Cinderella*
Ross Kemp	Henchman	*Snow White and the Seven Dwarfs*

TALES OF CHRISTMAS PAST

1925

I am dreadfully busy this year – it makes my hand more shaky than ever when I think of it – and not very rich. In fact, awful things have been happening, and some of the presents have got spoilt and I haven't got the North Polar Bear to help me and I have had to move house just before Christmas, so you can imagine what a state everything is in, and you will see why I have a new address. It all happened like this: one very windy day last November my hood blew off and went and stuck on the top of the North Pole. I told him not to, but the North Polar Bear climbed up to the thin top to get it down – and he did. The pole broke in the middle and fell on the roof of my house, and the North Polar Bear fell through the hole it made into the dining room with my hood over his nose, and all the snow fell off the roof into the house and melted and put out all the fires and ran down into the cellars where I was collecting this year's presents, and the North Polar Bear's leg got broken. He is well again now, but I was so cross with him that he says he won't try to help me again. I expect his temper is hurt, and will be mended by next Christmas. I send you a picture of the accident, and of my new house on the cliffs above the North Pole (with beautiful cellars in the cliffs). If John can't read my old shaky writing (1925 years old) he must get his father to. When is Michael going to learn to read, and write his own letters to me? Lots of love to you both and Christopher, whose name is rather like mine.

JRR Tolkien, *The Father Christmas Letters*, 1976

'Father Christmas' wrote letters to Tolkien's children, John, Michael, Christopher and Priscilla, every year between 1920 and 1942. In them, he described goings on at the North Pole, which grew to include appearances by North Polar Bear, Snow-elves, Red Gnomes, Snow-men, Cave-bears and the Polar Bear's nephews, Paksu and Valotukka.

WE THREE KINGS

We don't know for sure how many kings attended the birth of Christ, but we do know that in 1066, there were three kings in England. First came Edward the Confessor, who was crowned in 1042. Before his death on 4 January 1066, he named his successor as Harold, son of Godwine. However, Harold's crown was snatched by William, Duke of Normandy, who considered himself to be the true heir. Harold tried to defend his title but was killed at the Battle of Hastings on 14 October. William the Conqueror was crowned King of England on Christmas Day, 1066.

38 *Year in the 20th century that snow fell in the UK on Christmas Day, the first of only two records by the Met office that century*

CHRISTMAS DINNER IN... JAMAICA

On Christmas Day in Jamaica you could be tucking into:

Christmas Breakfast
Ackee (fruit related to lychee) and saltfish
Breadfruit
Fried plantains
Boiled bananas
Fresh fruit juice

Christmas Lunch
Fresh fruits
Sorrel
Rum punch
Meat

Christmas Dinner
Chicken
Curried goat
Stewed oxtail
Rice
Peas
Jamaican red wine and white rum fruitcake

HAVE YOURSELF A SWINGING CHRISTMAS

Some 1960s Christmas albums, singles and bootlegs from www.mistletunes.com

A Christmas Gift to You .... Phil Spector
Merry Christmas .... The Sonics, The Wailers and The Galaxies
The Beach Boys' Christmas Album .... The Beach Boys
Ultimate Christmas .... The Beach Boys
Merry Christmas and Happy New Year .... Jimi Hendrix
Christmastime is Here Again .... The Beatles
Complete Christmas Collection – 1963-1969 .... The Beatles
A Rock 'n' Roll Christmas..................... Various Artists
The Four Seasons Greetings.................. The Four Seasons
The Ventures' Christmas Album .... The Ventures
Rockin' Around the Christmas Tree .... Brenda Lee
Pretty Paper .... Roy Orbison

QUOTE UNQUOTE

A white Christmas fills the churchyard.
French proverb

SEASON'S GREETINGS

Sending Christmas cards has now become a habitual part of the season's festivities, but it wasn't always so.

Although ancient Roman 'New Year's cards' have been found in stone tablet form, it was a canny children's publisher, Sir Henry Cole, who first brought in commercial Christmas cards, in London in 1843.

The first card was printed in a batch of a thousand, with each copy on sale for a shilling each and featuring an illustration by John Callcott Horsley of a family drinking wine. The caption read: 'A Merry Christmas and a Happy New Year to you.'

The idea was a shrewd one considering that Cole had just helped introduce the Penny Post (the first pre-paid stamp system) a few years earlier: the more cards that were sent, the more profit was made. However, the image did cause some controversy, as the wine-scoffing family included a small child. The card didn't sell well and Cole left the Christmas card business for a more illustrious post as director of the Victoria and Albert Museum.

Subsequent early designs showed that people were less keen on winter or religious themes and more drawn to depictions that reminded the recipient of the imminent approach of spring: flowers, fairies and sentimental drawings of animals and children. Cards also took on more elaborate shapes and incorporated decorative techniques. By 1877 the first 'Post Early for Christmas' notices also appeared.

Christmas card collecting was a popular pastime and avid fans included Queen Mary, whose large collection is now housed in the British Museum. Cards from 'the golden age of printing' (around 1840-1890) are especially prized; one of Horsley's original designs sold for nearly £9,000 at an auction in 2005.

The first 'official' Christmas cards were also produced in the 1840s, starting in Queen Victoria's reign. This triggered a trend for British royal family cards showing portraits of the clan and reflecting personal events of the year (picture the late Queen Mother with her four grandchildren, Charles, Andrew, Edward and Anne, on a lawn somewhere). Over in the US, the first Presidential cards were introduced by Dwight D Eisenhower in 1953 and tend to depict White House scenes as rendered by prominent American artists.

Today, in the UK, we now send nearly 750,000 Christmas cards a year.

 Number of days after Christmas, on which Candlemas Day is celebrated – on 2 February

Little Thomas' list for Santa got longer every year. His parents didn't even know what a 'PlayStation' was.

INDULGE IN... MRS BEETON'S PLUM-PUDDING SAUCE

Advice on how best to prepare plum-pudding sauce, from Mrs Beeton's Book of Household Management *(1861) by Isabella Mary Mason Beeton:*

499

Ingredients – 1 wineglassful of brandy, 2oz. of very fresh butter, 1 glass of Madeira, pounded sugar to taste.

Mode: Put the pounded sugar in a basin, with part of the brandy and the butter; let it stand by the side of the fire until it is warm and the sugar and butter are dissolved; then add the rest of the brandy, with the Madeira. Either pour it over the pudding, or serve in a tureen. This is a very rich and excellent sauce.

Average cost: 1s. 3d. for this quantity.
Sufficient for a pudding made for 6 persons.

Year in the 19th century when Prince Albert first brought a Christmas tree back from Germany and put it in Windsor Castle

MERRY MAGNA CARTA

The Christmas of 1214 goes down in history as the year in which the barons of England demanded that King John sign a charter of English liberties – the *Magna Carta* or Great Charter. During his reign, King John's tyranny and lawlessness had become intolerable and the people's hope hung on the French campaign in which he was engaged. When John lost the Battle of Bouvines in July 1214, this gave strength to his opponents. This prompted the barons of England to meet in secret in Edmundsbury where they agreed to demand from him, with force if needed, the restoration of their liberties by charter under the king's seal. When Christmas Day came, John was at Worcester, attended only by a few of his immediate staff and some foreign mercenaries. It was customary for the barons to visit at Christmas and offer their congratulations but none came. John was alarmed by their absence and hastily rode to London and shut himself in the house of the Knights Templar. While there, the barons assembled in London and, on the Feast of Epiphany, they presented themselves in arms before the king to demand his confirmation of the laws of Edward the Confessor and Henry I. At first, John met their requests with refusal and threats. However, they stood firm and he was eventually forced to sign the Great Charter at a conference in Runnymede in 1215. The most important clauses of the charter protect the personal liberty and property of every freeman in the kingdom by giving security from arbitrary imprisonment and unjust exactions. A good Christmas gift if ever there was one.

BOXING DAY DIP

Swimming in the sea on Boxing Day might sound like a breeze if you're in Australia or Thailand, but would you brave the North Sea? Over 1,000 dippers and 5,000 spectators think it's a great idea and even dress up for the event at Seaburn Beach near Sunderland. Originating in 1974, this fundraising Boxing Day Dip is organised by the Lions Club of Sunderland and is one of the oldest events of its type in the country. Another famous 'dip' is organised by the North Sea Volunteer Lifeguards (NSVL), taking its brave participants into the brisk waters of Whitley Bay. With sea temperatures ranging anywhere from 4-10°C, the main challenge doesn't actually seem to be to swim anywhere but to out-dip the cold. For those who do, Christmas dinner leftovers have probably never tasted so good.

42 *Percentage of Brits who were estimated to be working over the festive period, according to research by Fujitsu Computers in 2005*

QUOTE UNQUOTE

A Christmas shopper's complaint is one of long-standing.
Jay Leno, US TV presenter and comedian

THE NATIVITY: MARY

Some things you may or may not know about principal characters in the Nativity:

- The name Mary comes from the Hebrew name Miriam
- Mary is known from the New Testament of the canonical Bible as the mother of Jesus
- Important Nativity events for Mary, as told in the canonical Gospels, include the Annunciation of Jesus' conception, Mary's visit to Elizabeth, Mary's journey to Bethlehem and Jesus' birth in a manger
- The New Testament describes her as a young maiden although the Greek word *parthénos* was used and this traditionally signifies an actual virgin
- The New Testament tells us that Mary was conceived by the agency of the Holy Spirit while she was already the betrothed wife of Joseph of the House of David
- Some Christians maintain that Mary was a virgin at the point of conception and at least until the birth of Jesus; others that she remained a virgin for the rest of her life
- Unlike Joseph, Mary is recounted in the New Testament as being present at various important stages of Jesus' adult life: for example, at the Wedding at Cana, at his crucifixion and at communal prayers immediately after Jesus' Ascension
- Even though Mary is present at Jesus' crucifixion, we are never told that she cradles the dead body of her son although this is a common motif in art
- In later Christian apocrypha, Mary's parents' names are given as Joachim and Anne
- Mary's death is not recorded in scripture but tradition has her assumed or taken bodily into heaven when her tomb is found empty by the Apostles
- A chapter in the Qur'an is titled Maryam, in which the story of Mary and Jesus is recounted according to the Islamic view of Jesus
- Mary is often depicted as wearing blue and white clothes, but an actual description of her appearance is never given in the Bible

Year in the 19th century that the first Christmas card was created, on the instructions of Sir Henry Cole

CHRISTMAS ISLAND: KIRITIMATI

There are several Christmas Islands in the world – and thankfully for the residents and wildlife there, these islands do exist all year round…

Name of island: Kiritimati
Nationality: Republic of Kiribati
Location: Pacific Ocean, 232km north of the Equator, 6,700km from Sydney and 5,360km from San Francisco

This Christmas Island forms part of the Line Islands and also the Republic of Kiribati in the Pacific Ocean. When Westerners first came here, it appeared to be uninhabited. However, there may have been a small or temporary native population, probably made up of traders and settlers. They may have stopped here and on other Line Islands on their way from the Society Islands to Hawaii between around AD400 and AD1000.

Captain James Cook officially discovered Kiritimati on Christmas Eve 1777. However, it was then claimed by the United States under the Guano Islands Acts of 1856 with permanent settlement recorded as starting by 1882. Settlers were mainly coconut plantation workers and fishermen, although an extreme drought led to a forced abandonment of the island between 1905 and 1912.

A French priest, Father Emmanuel Rougier, leased the island from 1917 to 1939 and planted some 800,000 coconut trees there. The island was then occupied by the Allies in World War II, providing rest and refuelling facilities for planes travelling between Hawaii and the South Pacific.

The war theme continued with some nuclear testing during the Cold War. Indeed, the British supposedly conducted their first successful hydrogen bomb test at Malden Island in 1957, with Kiritimati as the operation's main base. Although this test is now known to have been a failure, the first British H-Bomb was successfully detonated over the southeastern tip of Kiritimati on 8 November 1957. The island was then proposed as a suitable launch site for manned spacecraft – for example, the Japanese *HOPE-X* space shuttle. The US then conducted 22 successful nuclear detonations as part of Operation Dominic in 1962. By 1969 military interest in the island finally ceased with facilities converted for civilian use.

Today the entire island is a designated wildlife sanctuary, although marine, bird and land wildlife here has been seriously thwarted by continuous human intervention and damage by El Niño in the 1980s.

Kiritimati is also the first inhabited place on Earth to experience the New Year each year, with a 1995 realignment of the International Dateline 'moving' the island from the east of the meridian to the west. Christmas, of course, is here all year round.

 Number of Christmas songs and carols for children from around the world, contained in the book Merrily to Bethlehem

CHRISTMAS IN PICTURES

'Hello, is that Argos? Please could I have 30,000 LEGO sets by Friday?'

SANTA'S CHIMNEY

In 1927, Alexander Woolcott, Franklin Pierce Adams, George Kaufman, Robert Benchley and Dorothy Parker gathered for an NBC Red radio network Christmas special. Lured to the table by the promise of free drinks, they appeared unaware that they were live on air. Instead of witty seasonal banter, they launched into a trashing of Edna Ferber's latest novel *Mother Knows Best*. They then complained about their diminutive sex lives. And in the 23rd minute Dorothy Parker, now on her fifth drink, finally added a seasonal quip with the line 'one more of these and I'll be sliding down Santa's chimney'. Cue for the feed to be cut, quicksmart.

TALES OF CHRISTMAS PAST

"...I like dreams, and have a great many curious ones myself. But they don't keep me from being tired of Christmas," said Effie, poking discontentedly among the sweeties for something worth eating.

"Why are you tired of what should be the happiest time of all the year?" asked mamma, anxiously.

"Perhaps I shouldn't be if I had something new. But it is always the same, and there isn't any more surprise about it. I always find heaps of goodies in my stocking. Don't like some of them, and soon get tired of those I do like. We always have a great dinner, and I eat too much, and feel ill next day. Then there is a Christmas tree somewhere, with a doll on top, or a stupid old Santa Claus, and children dancing and screaming over bonbons and toys that break, and shiny things that are of no use. Really, mamma, I've had so many Christmases all alike that I don't think I can bear another one." And Effie laid herself flat on the sofa, as if the mere idea was too much for her.

Her mother laughed at her despair, but was sorry to see her little girl so discontented, when she had everything to make her happy, and had known but ten Christmas days.

Louisa May Alcott, *A Christmas Dream*, 1886

THE CHRISTMAS CUBE

In July 2008, Woolworths tipped the Rubik's Cube to top the Christmas bestsellers list once again, more than 25 years after its launch. The cube fell out of favour in the 1990s but is experiencing a revival, thanks to tutorials on YouTube and speedcubing, which is where people compete to match the colours. Over 300 million cubes have been sold since the toy's launch in 1980 but no matter how many cubes you have there is still only one answer. As a homage to the cube, a poetic quote from its inventor Erno Rubik is certain to add weight to Woolworths' claim about the cube gaining fans this Christmas. Describing how he invented the cube, he said: 'It was wonderful, to see how, after only a few turns, the colours became mixed, apparently in random fashion. It was tremendously satisfying to watch this colour parade. Like after a nice walk when you have seen many lovely sights you decide to go home, after a while I decided it was time to go home, let us put the cubes back in order. And it was at that moment that I came face to face with the Big Challenge: What is the way home?' A question many people will be asking this Christmas, no doubt, when they find a cube in their stocking.

 Year in the 19th century that Christmas crackers were invented by Thomas Smith

AN APPLE A CHRISTMAS DAY...

Some of the myths and superstitions that surround Christmas...

An apple a day keeps the doctor away. An apple on Christmas Eve will give you good health for the year to come

Don't want to lose a friend before next Christmas? Eat plum pudding on Christmas Day

On Christmas Eve it is said that all animals can speak. But, it is bad luck to test this superstition

A child born on Christmas Day will have good luck

Wearing new shoes on Christmas Day will bring bad luck

Eat a raw egg first thing on Christmas morning and you'll be able to lift heavy weights

Don't refuse a mince pie at Christmas dinner or you will have bad luck for the coming day. The amount of luck you have in the coming months depends on how many houses you eat mince pies in – one happy month for each house

A white Christmas will bring a green Easter

Place shoes by side on Christmas Eve to prevent family arguments. Or if in Greece, burn old shoes to prevent bad luck in the coming year

A starry, starry night on Christmas Eve will bring good crops in summer

Devonshire girls should rap on the henhouse door on Christmas Eve. If a rooster crows, you will marry within the year

Shout 'Christmas Gift' to your first Christmas Day visitor and they must give you a gift

QUOTE UNQUOTE

I'm dreaming of a white Christmas,
Just like the ones I used to know,
Where the tree tops glisten
And children listen
To hear sleigh bells in the snow.
From the song 'White Christmas' by Irving Berlin,
first sung by Bing Crosby in the film *Holiday Inn*

Year in the 20th century in which Oslo first sent a Christmas tree to London, in thanks for British help during World War II 47

THE NATIVITY: A STARRING ROLE

Well-known films that portray the Nativity include:

Ben Hur, 1959
The Greatest Story Ever Told, 1965
Jesus of Nazareth (TV), 1977
The Nativity (TV), 1978
Monty Python's Life of Brian, 1979
The Nativity Story, 2006

CHRISTMAS CRACKERS

The ones you wish you'd never pulled...

JOKE: What do you call people who are afraid of Santa Claus?

Answer on page 153

FESTIVE FLORA AND FAUNA: THE ROBIN

The robin adorns many a Christmas card and decoration throughout the festive season. Most people believe that the robin's inclusion in Christmas festivities is due to its more prominent and prolific appearance in midwinter, when a shortage of food makes it tame and puff out its feathers against the cold. The robin's orangey-red breast is also highly distinctive, especially against a snowy or grey background, giving birth to the name 'robin redbreast' in the 15th century. In ancient Norse mythology the robin was held to be a storm-cloud bird and sacred to Thor, the god of thunder. His association with Christmas began in the 19th century when the first Christmas cards appeared and the robin's image seemed like an ideal jolly figurehead for festivities. He was also said to represent Victorian postmen, who delivered the cards dressed in their customary red uniforms also earning them the nickname 'Robin'. However, some Christians also claim that the robin acquired its colouring when one punctured its breast trying to pluck the thorns from Christ's head at the crucifixion. Others say it happened when the robin sang into Christ's ear to try and comfort him and the blood that dripped down stained his breast. A further legend goes that the robin scorched its breast while trying to fetch water for souls in Purgatory. Even if you just believe the red feathers are there for purely decorative or territorial purposes, the robin looks set to stick around at Christmas time.

 Year in the 19th century in which the popular carol 'Once in Royal David's City' was written

THE ART OF THE ORNAMENT

Every year since 1988, The Tate has commissioned a leading contemporary artist to design its Christmas Tree. It is then exhibited in the Rotunda – the glass-domed hall and gallery of the Tate Britain. Twenty years on we can compare the trees across three decades, many symbolising issues that were important at the time:

1988 Bill Woodrow

The first of the trees decorated by an artist, ornaments comprised about 30 cardboard sculptures with a large illuminated globe hanging above the tree. The use of maps in the decorations reinforced the suggestion of a theme that concerned itself with the condition of the world at the time, and presented an ecological view of the planet.

1998 Richard Wilson

Wilson didn't want a conventional Christmas tree. Instead he made a sculpture using industrial and found materials to express both the order and the chaos of Christmas. The structure of the tree was formed of basic workshop-style shelving units. These units were then decorated with functional storage boxes in bright primary colours, reminiscent of Christmas gifts, and with bare electric light bulbs in wire cages. Within the framework hung a metal artificial tree, skeletal like the shelves and originally covered in glitter. The tree was designed to evoke both the glamour of Christmas and the empty materialism so often beneath it.

See the Christmas trees at
www.tate.org.uk/britain/exhibitions/christmastree

RALLY THE WRENBOYS

Some take the St Stephen's Day (Boxing Day) tradition of Hunting the Wren very seriously, not least those who have written and published songs to help keep the custom alive. They include:

- Liam Clancy, who recorded 'The Wren Song' in 1955 – this was then sung by wrenboys in Ireland
- Steeleye Span, who recorded a wren song called 'The King' in 1972, on the album *Please to See the King*
- John Kirkpatrick, who recorded the song 'Hunting the Wren' on his album *Wassail!*
- The Chieftains, who also made a collection of wrenboy tunes on their album *Bells of Dublin*

Year in the 17th century that the first American Christmas carol was written – 'Jesus is Born', by John de Brebeur

SANTA BY ANY OTHER NAME

Some gift giving and Christmas figureheads from around the world...

Afghanistan	Baba Chaghaloo
Albania	Babadimri
Armenia	Kaghand Papik
Austria	Weihnachtsmann
	Christkind
Brazil	Papai Noel/Os
	Três Reis Magos
Bulgaria	Dyado Koleda
Canada	Santa Claus
Chile	Viejito Pascuero
China	Shengdan Laoren
	Sing Dan Lo Yan
Cornwall	Tas Nadelik
Croatia	Djed Mraz
Denmark	Julemanden
Egypt	Papa Noël
Ecuador	Papa Noel
Estonia	Jöuluvana
Finland	Joulupukki
France	Père Noël
Germany	Weihnachtsmann
	Christkind
Hungary	Milulás
	J´zuska
	Kis Jézus
	Télapó
Iceland	Jólasveinninn
Indonesia	Sinterklas
Iran	Baba Noel
Ireland	Daidi na Nollag
	Santa Claus
Italy	Babbo Natale
	La Befana
	Santa Lucia
Lebanon	Baba Noel
Liechtenstein	Christkind
Macedonia	Dedo Mraz
Malta	San Niklaw
	Santa Klaws
Mexico	Santo Clós
	El Niño Dios
	Los Reyes Magos
Netherlands	Kerstman
Norway	Julenissen
Pakistan	Christmas Baba
Philippines	Santa Klaus
Poland	Gwiazdor
Portugal	Pai Natal
	Menino Jesus
Russia	Ded Moroz
South Africa	Vade Kersfees
	Sinterklaas
	Father Christmas
	Santa Claus
Spain	Reyes Magos
	Papá Noel
Sri Lanka	Naththal Seeya
Sweden	Jultomen
Switzerland	Samichlaus
	Christkind
	Babbo Natale
	Père Noël
Turkey	Noel Baba
UK	Father Christmas
	Santa Claus
US	Santa Claus
	Kris Kringle
	St Nicholas
	St Nick
Wales	Siôn Corn

QUOTE UNQUOTE

I stopped believing in Santa Claus when I was six. Mother took me to see him in a department store and he asked for my autograph.
Shirley Temple, US actress

50 *Per cent chance of Cleveland, Ohio, getting a white Christmas in 2007 according to the National Climatic Data Center's survey of 350 US cities*

A BOOK IS NOT JUST FOR CHRISTMAS...

Stuck for stocking fillers? Why not adopt a book from the British Library and help conserve some of the 150 million books, manuscripts, newspapers and other items in its collections? You can choose from various titles at www.bl.uk/adoptabook, including:

A Christmas Carol (Charles Dickens)	1934
Christmas Number of All the Year Round (Wilkie Collins)	1878
The British Baker's Selected Recipes	c1900
The Lady's Bazaar and Fancy Fair Book	1875
First World War Christmas Cards	1914-1918

AWAY IN A MANGER?

A common Christmas Nativity scene is the Baby Jesus in a manger because there is 'no room at the inn'. Here's how the Bible tells it:

The Gospels of St Matthew and St Luke both state that Jesus was born in Bethlehem but neither states exactly where he was born. Luke tells us that Joseph and Mary had travelled to Bethlehem for the Census of Quirinius, because this was the town of Joseph's ancestors, the birthplace of David. Because of the census, we can derive that the town was very busy with other visitors making the same journey as Joseph. Luke then tells us that Mary gave birth to Jesus and laid him in a manger (from the Greek word *phatne* for a trough or stall used to hold food for animals) because there was no place for them in the inn.

In fact, the word for inn is translated from the Greek word *kataluma*. This could mean inn or guestroom and some scholars have speculated that Joseph and Mary may have actually sought to stay with relatives as their 'guest', only to find that their house was full. They may then have resorted to the shelter of a room with a manger.

In Western art, the manger is usually depicted as being in a man-made freestanding structure. In Byzantine art, the manger is often positioned in a cave, carved in the side of a hill. In classical Palestine – where Bethlehem is located today – this was the typical location of stables. The Church of the Nativity in Bethlehem – built over the place that tradition marks as the birthplace of Christ and one of the oldest continuously operating churches in the world – is also built over a cave.

While scholars are still arguing the point, it may be interesting to take your Nativity play back to the cave, stone manger and all, although it's worth discussing with your props department first.

Year in the 19th century in which the popular Christmas carol 'O Little Town of Bethlehem' was written

BIRDS OF A FEATHER

In the UK, turkey is widely considered to be the most traditional bird to appear on the Christmas table, but it wasn't always so.

While large, stuffed fowl has been part and parcel of the Christmas feast for centuries, like many other Christian holiday food traditions, this custom has been borrowed from earlier cultural practices. In feasting terms, the larger the bird, the more festive the presence and the more prestige would be reflected.

The peacock was an especially fine show for a festive occasion at the medieval dinner table of the wealthy and the noble, only superseded by the swan. Goose was also a fine figure of a bird on celebratory tables and is again enjoying a Christmas dinner revival. In the Middle Ages, geese were traditionally eaten twice a year, once as a young goose in summer and again as a fattened bird at Michaelmas – now celebrated on 29 September.

The feast of Michaelmas was associated with autumn and the shortening of days and the goose represented seasonal harvest; the migratory bird would appear several times a year. The Michaelmas roast goose tradition is also a perpetuation of Celtic Samhain ceremonies or Halloween, and Germanic Yule, originally the first day of the New Year.

At the height of their popularity in Britain, Goose Clubs were even set up into which less wealthy citizens could pay a sum in order to secure some goose meat for Christmas. This is illustrated in Charles Dickens' *A Christmas Carol* and in Sir Arthur Conan Doyle's Sherlock Holmes short story *The Adventure of the Blue Carbuncle*.

Meanwhile, over in North America, early American settlers found that turkeys were more plentiful than geese and so began to serve these at Michaelmas, Christmas and their other big feasting event – Thanksgiving.

The turkey then found its way from the New World via Spanish ships that were travelling back from Mexico. They presented the bird as a gift to Spain, from where it made its way to the Spanish Netherlands and finally to England in the 16th century. Great turkey farms were then set up in East Anglia to provide fodder for the tables of the wealthy.

A common Christmas dinner tradition today is to use the turkey's wishbone to make a wish. Two people pull opposite ends of the wishbone, until it breaks, with the person holding the larger fragment of the bone winning the game. Not so easy, one imagines, with the wishbone of a peacock…

 Height in feet of the Capitol Christmas Tree in Washington, in 1983, 1979 and 1977

CHRISTMAS IN PICTURES

Young Albert usually found that once the charades were in full swing, no one noticed him polishing off the mulled wine.

HAVING AN EPIPHANY

Ways in which it is said that some people still celebrate Epiphany – usually 6 January – around the world...

Europe	Taking the greenery from Christmas down
France	Eating *gâteau* or *galette des Rois*
Mexico	Polishing shoes and leaving them out for presents the night before along with a letter to the Three Kings; the shoes are filled with hay for the camels
Portugal	Eating *bolo Rei*
Puerto Rico	Leaving a hay-filled box under the bed for presents
Spain	Polishing shoes and leaving them out for presents the night before; leaving sweet wine, fruit and nibbles for the camels

THE NATIVITY, STARRING POSH AND BECKS

David Beckham as Joseph, Victoria Beckham as Mary, Graham Norton, Samuel L Jackson and Hugh Grant as shepherds, Kylie Minogue as an angel and Tony Blair and George Bush as wise men? This is the scene that met hundreds of visitors to Madame Tussauds waxworks museum in December 2004. Displayed in the 'Divas' hall of the museum, the celebrity crèche looked out onto the likes of J-Lo and Beyoncé. Instead of carols or Christmas songs, the scene was completed by professional dancers, grooving to the music of Britney Spears. Many tourists found the scene comical and happily posed for pictures alongside the waxy celebrities. However, it was reported that the Vatican was not amused, an official spokesman telling Reuters in Rome that: 'It is worse than bad taste. It is cheap… You cannot use contemporary personalities as the central figures in the Nativity… and it becomes worse, if that were possible, if the people may be of questionable moral standing.' A spokesman for the Archbishop of Canterbury reacted with rather more wearied resignation saying: 'There is a tradition of each generation trying to reinterpret the Nativity but, oh dear…' Madame Tussauds stood by their Nativity, having run a poll of 300 visitors to the attraction to see which celebrities they would most like in the scene. Posh and Becks came out overwhelmingly on top. Only the baby Jesus was spared ridicule, being represented by a plastic doll. Not unlike some of the other chosen ones then…

FESTIVE FLORA AND FAUNA: POINSETTIAS

Otherwise known as Mexican flame leaf, Christmas star and winter rose, the poinsettia is a species of plant indigenous to Mexico and native to the Pacific coast of the US. Under their most common title, they are named after Joel Robert Poinsett, the first United States Ambassador to Mexico, who introduced the plant to the US in 1825. In ancient times, the Aztecs used the plant to produce a red dye and fever-reducing medicine. The plant's association with Christmas then originated in 16th-century Mexico, where a little girl who was too poor to provide a gift to celebrate Christ's birthday instead gathered a bunch of weeds by the roadside. She is said to have placed these on the church altar and from the weeds were said to sprout the crimson blossom of poinsettia. Franciscan monks in Mexico, struck by the legend, introduced the plants into their Christmas celebrations. Poinsettias are now an international symbol of Christmas and in the US, 12 December is National Poinsettia Day.

 Year in the 20th century that the film White Christmas, *starring Bing Crosby and Danny Kaye, was first aired*

TO TREE OR NOT TO TREE

The Christmas tree is not without its controversy, with some Christians finding direction in the Bible for not celebrating with one. As spoken in Jeremiah 10:1-5 in the King James version...

Hear ye the word which the Lord speaketh unto you, O house of Israel: Thus saith the Lord, Learn not the way of the heathen, and be not dismayed at the signs of heaven; for the heathen are dismayed at them. For the customs of the people are vain: for one cutteth a tree out of the forest, the work of the hands of the workman, with the axe. They deck it with silver and with gold; they fasten it with nails and with hammers, that it move not. They are upright as the palm tree, but speak not: they must needs be borne, because they cannot go. Be not afraid of them; for they cannot do evil, neither also is it in them to do good.

CHRISTMAS CRACKERS

The ones you wish you'd never pulled...

JOKE: Who is never hungry at Christmas?

Answer on page 153

CHRISTMAS DINNER IN... THE USA

On Christmas Day in the USA you could be tucking into:

- Turkey, ham or roast beef
- Stuffing (commonly called dressing)
- Cranberry sauce
- Corn
- Squash
- Green beans
- Pumpkin pie
- Marzipan
- *Pfeffernusse* (small, hard, round biscuits with spices including pepper)
- Sugar cookies
- *Panettone* (Milanese sweet bread with candied fruit and raisins)
- Turkey teriyaki (Hawaii)
- Oysters and ham pie (Virginia)
- Lutefisk (Upper Midwest)
- *Bischochito* (crisp butter cookie flavoured with anise and cinnamon, common in New Mexico)

Weight in jumbo jets that the Woodland Trust estimates is equivalent to that produced by Christmas card waste in the UK each year 55

SANTA'S LITTLE HELPERS: BELSNICKEL

Luckily for Santa, delivering all the presents at Christmas isn't just up to him and his tribe of elves and reindeer – a whole troop of gift-givers are out and about spreading their joy. As long as you've been a good little girl or boy that is...

Similar to Krampus in Austria and Germany, Belsnickel is a Dutch mythical being who visits children at Christmastime. Introduced to the Middle American colonies by 19th-century German immigrants, he is something of a dour character, dressed in dark or shaggy clothing or in fur and skins with a tall, pointed hood. Until late in the century, he would visit German houses in Baltimore and Pennsylvania on Christmas Eve, carrying a bundle of switches for naughty children and treats for the good ones. Subsequently, Belsnickel was not well loved except by parents wanting to keep their children in line. In more lenient households, he was accompanied by St Nicholas or Christkindl who came to spread joy and peace to the world. Today, the tradition of Belsnickel is more likely to be served up as figurines imported from Germany in the form of toys, decorations and chocolate moulds.

QUOTE UNQUOTE

Christmas is the season for kindling the fire of hospitality in the hall, the genial flame of charity in the heart.
Washington Irving, US author and historian

TALES OF CHRISTMAS PAST

From the Christmas Day 1835 entry

CHRISTMAS-DAY.–In a few more days, the fourth year of our absence from England will be completed. Our first Christmas-day was spent at Plymouth; the second at St Martin's Cove, near Cape Horn; the third at Port Desire, in Patagonia; the fourth at anchor in a harbour in the Peninsula of Tres Montes; this fifth here; and the next, I trust in providence, will be in England. We attended divine service in the chapel of Paihia; part of the service was read in English, and part in the New Zealand language.

Charles Darwin, *Journal of Researches into the geology and natural history of the various countries visited by HMS Beagle, under the command of Captain Fitzroy RN from 1832 to 1836* (commonly known as '*The Voyage of the Beagle*'), 1839

56 *Number in millions of Christmas tree seedlings planted every year in the US, according to the National Christmas Tree Association*

IT'S THE GRAFT THAT COUNTS

A 2003 article in the *International Herald Tribune* related an event covered about New York in an edition some hundred years back in December 1903. The report titled 'A Strange Christmas Gift' read that Eva Doniger, 16, gave her brother Jacob, 23, a very special Christmas gift that year. Eva went home early on 24 December, telling her sisters that she had given up her position in a department store. 'Because I want to take my Christmas present to Jacob,' she explained. In fact, she had made arrangements for the physicians of Bellevue to take 10 inches of skin from her and graft it on to her brother – a very thoughtful gift indeed and one that brought the siblings even closer together.

HOW THE GRINCH WAS STOLEN FROM CHRISTMAS

Parodies of Dr Seuss' miserly character The Grinch – he who stole Christmas – in popular and contemporary culture...

'How the Grinch Stole Congress'	A feature in *The Nation* magazine, 1994
'How the Grinch Stole the Election'	A satire by humorist Bill Maher in the 2000 elections
'How the Sith Stole Christmas'	An internet animation by Ted Bracewell combining elements of *The Grinch* with *Star Wars*
'A Hero Sits Next Door'	The Grinch takes on a cameo role in a *Family Guy* episode
'Merry Christmas Charlie Manson'	The Grinch appears as The Grinchiepoo in a *South Park* episode
'Last Exit to Springfield'	Mr Burns recites a snippet of Seuss-like rhyming verse in the style of The Grinch in an episode of *The Simpsons*
'Tis the Fifteenth Season'	Homer breaks into everyone's homes and steals the gifts given by Ned Flanders while singing the tune 'You're a Mean One, Mr Grinch' in an episode of *The Simpsons*
'Kill Gil: Vols 1 & 2'	The Grinch is parodied as The Grumple in an episode of *The Simpsons*

Year in the 20th century that the Queen's Christmas speech was televised for the first time 57

HAVE AN EPIPHANY

There are many traditions associated with the Epiphany, or the traditional day on which the arrival of the Magi is celebrated. This is accepted as 6 January each year. You could extend the Christmas season by:

- Sending wish letters to the Three Kings on the night before Epiphany
- Leave a drink out for the Magi and food for their camels
- Organise a Spanish *cabalgatas*, in which the 'kings' and 'servants' parade and throw sweets to children attending
- Write the initials of the Three Kings above the main door of your house to confer blessings for the coming year. This could be performed, as in some parts of Germany and Austria, by children carrying a star
- Follow French and Belgian customs and bake a cake containing a bean. Whoever finds the bean should be crowned king for the day
- Follow the above but add a Spanish twist, by baking or buying a ring-shaped pastry called a *Roscón de Reyes*. Along with the bean, hide a small figurine of the Baby Jesus. Whoever finds Jesus is crowned the king, whoever finds the bean must pay for the cost of the cake
- Following the tradition for *Roscón de Reyes*, but do it the Mexican way. Whoever finds the Baby Jesus must buy tamales for the Candelaria feast on 2 February

TALES OF CHRISTMAS PAST

Christmas Eve

As we approached the house, we heard the sound of music, and now and then a burst of laughter, from one end of the building. This, Bracebridge said must proceed from the servants' hall, where a great deal of revelry was permitted, and even encouraged by the squire, throughout the twelve days of Christmas, provided every thing was done conformably to ancient usage. Here were kept up the old games of hoodman blind, shoe the wild mare, hot cockles, steal the white loaf, bob apple, and snap dragon: the Yule clog and Christmas candle were regularly burnt, and the mistletoe, with its white berries, hung up, to the imminent peril of all the pretty housemaids.

So intent were the servants upon their sports that we had to ring repeatedly before we could make ourselves heard.

Washington Irving, *Old Christmas: from the sketch-book of Washington Irving*, 1886

58 *Number in millions of Christmas cards recycled by the Woodland Trust in 2005, as part of their annual campaign – equivalent to 1,150 tonnes*

CHRISTMAS ISLAND DISCS

Singers, songwriters and musicians who have written songs and produced albums under the name 'Christmas Island'...

Depeche Mode
Jimmy Buffett
Leon Redbone
Petta Booka
The Andrews Sisters

QUOTE UNQUOTE

If Ifs and Buts were candies and nuts,
we'd all have a merry Christmas.
Unknown

MAKE ROOM FOR... MRS BEETON'S CHRISTMAS CAKE

Advice on how best to prepare Christmas cake, from Mrs Beeton's Book of Household Management *(1861) by Isabella Mary Mason Beeton (1836-1865):*

1754

Ingredients: 5 teacupfuls of flour, 1 teacupful of melted butter, 1 teacupful of cream, 1 teacupful of treacle, 1 teacupful of moist sugar, 2 eggs, ½ oz. of powdered ginger, ½ lb. of raisins, 1 teaspoonful of carbonate of soda, 1 tablespoonful of vinegar.

Mode: Make the butter sufficiently warm to melt it, but do not allow it to oil; put the flour into a basin; add to it the sugar, ginger, and raisins, which should be stoned and cut into small pieces. When these dry ingredients are thoroughly mixed, stir in the butter, cream, treacle, and well-whisked eggs, and beat the mixture for a few minutes. Dissolve the soda in the vinegar, add it to the dough, and be particular that these latter ingredients are well incorporated with the others; put the cake into a buttered mould or tin, place it in a moderate oven immediately, and bake it from 1–¾ to 2–¼ hours.

Time: 1–¾ to 2–¼ hours.
Average cost: 1s. 6d.

Number of the street in New York at 6th Avenue, where you can find the Wollman Skating Rink in Central Park, a popular Christmas haunt

CHRISTMAS DINNER IN... GERMANY

On Christmas Day in Germany you could be tucking into:

- Roast goose
- Macaroni salad
- Marzipan
- *Reisbrei* (porridge)
- *Lebkuchen* (spiced cookie bars)
- *Stollen* (several types of bread including *Christstollen*)
- Suckling pig
- *Weisswurst* (traditional Bavarian 'white' sausage of minced veal and pork bacon)

CHRISTMAS CRACKERS

The ones you wish you'd never pulled...

JOKE: How do sheep greet each other at Christmas?

Answer on page 153

CAN YOU DIRECT ME TO JERUSALEM?

Yes. Jerusalem is situated around 31°47'N, 35°13'E on the southern spur of a plateau in the Judean Mountains. This mountain range includes the Mount of Olives and Mount Scopus. This makes the elevation of the Old City approximately 760m high, and leaves the whole of Jerusalem surrounded by valleys and dry riverbeds, including the Kidron, the Hinnom and the Tyropoeon Valleys. Jerusalem is 60km east of Tel Aviv and the Mediterranean Sea. It is also 35km from the Dead Sea, the lowest body of water on Earth. Neighbouring cities and towns include Bethlehem, the accepted birthplace of Christ – just a 20-minute drive away, Beit Jala, Abu Dis, Ma'ale Adumin, Mevaseret Zion, Ramallah and Giv'at Ze'ev. The city is sacred to three religions and home to three of the world's most venerated institutions: the Church of the Holy Sepulchre, held to be the location of the crucifixion of Christ, and the holiest site for Christians; the Western (Wailing) Wall, last remnant of the Second Temple and most sacred Jewish relic; and the Dome of the Rock, the third most hallowed location for Muslims, being the spot where Prophet Muhammad made his night ascent into heaven.

THE TWELVE DAYS OF CHRISTMAS

'On the first day of Christmas my true love gave to me...' – while the popular Christmas song 'The Twelve Days of Christmas' might sound like a romantic ditty, some believe that it was written as a mnemonic for English Catholics to teach the faith to their children when Catholicism was illegal in England. The symbolism is thought to go a little something like this:

My true love	God
Me	Believer of the Catholic faith
A partridge in a pear tree	Jesus Christ on the cross
Two turtledoves	The New and Old Testaments of the Holy Bible
Three French hens	The Three Theological Virtues: faith, hope and charity
Four calling birds	The Gospels of Matthew, Mark, Luke and John
Five golden rings	Pentateuch, the first five books of the Old Testament
Six geese-a-laying	The six days of creation
Seven swans-a-swimming	The Seven Sacraments
Eight maids-a-milking	The Eight Beatitudes
Nine ladies dancing	The nine fruits of the Holy Spirit:
Ten lords-a-leaping	The Ten Commandments
Eleven pipers piping	The eleven faithful Apostles of Jesus Christ
Twelve drummers drumming	The twelve points of principle of the Apostle's Creed

KNEEL BEFORE THE LORD

The Christian tradition of kneeling for prayer and worship could have stemmed from St Luke's description of the Nativity in the canonical Bible. His text states that upon meeting Jesus, the Magi – often referred to as the Three Kings – hand over their gifts and 'fall down' in joyous praise. This is thought to refer to them lying prostrate on the ground. In ancient Jewish and Roman tradition, kneeling and prostration were thought of as undignified. However, in Persia – where many people believe the Magi came from – it was a sign of great respect, often bestowed on a king. Through the kneeling and prostration in Luke's Nativity, these acts were adopted in the early Church and are still used in worship today.

Percentage of women likely to splash out on kids at Christmas, more than double that of men, according to a 2001 shopping survey by Microsoft

STIR IT UP

Love it or loath it, Christmas pudding isn't just about the eating, half the fun is in the stirring up...

For traditionalists, Christmas pudding doesn't just provide a fruitful end to turkey and all the trimmings. It all begins on Stir-Up Sunday, the last Sunday before Advent, considered to be the last day on which one can make Christmas puddings in order for them to taste as rich and regal as they should.

The custom goes that all family members must take a hand in the stirring using a special wooden spoon. The stirring must be done in a clockwise direction, with eyes shut, while making a secret wish of goodwill. The pudding is then steamed for many hours and left to mature. Some say the ingredients and recipe allow it to keep so well that you could make it a year before.

This is said to be connected to Church of England collects (a short prayer connected to a particular day or season) where churchgoers would utter the words: 'Stir up, we beseech thee, O Lord, the wills of thy faithful people, what they plenteously bring forth the fruit of good works.' This prayer was parodied by choirboys who sang: 'Stir up, we beseech thee, the pudding in the pot. And when we get home tonight, we'll eat it up hot.'

The pudding's origins can be traced back to the 1420s, although it took its final form in Victorian England. The first reference to 'Christmas Pudding' comes in Victorian chef Eliza Acton's *Modern Cookery for Private Families*, published in 1845. This pudding contained 4.5lb of dried fruit and candied peel, 16 eggs, 1 pint of brandy and 2lb of beef kidney suet. Her light 'cheap and good' option replaces the suet with 1lb of mashed potatoes, 1lb of boiled carrots and just 2lb of dried fruit.

This recipe harks back to the history of the Christmas pudding, first as a 15th-century pottage made from chopped beef or mutton, onions, root vegetables and dried fruit. The invention of the pudding cloth took the pottage from gravy form to the round pudding shape we associate with the Christmas pud today. Then, in the 16th century, new kinds of fruit were added including raisins and prunes and hence the plum (actually referring to the prune) pudding was born.

The meat was phased out in favour of suet and the root vegetables disappeared. By its savoury nature, this pudding was served as a first course rather than a dessert, also adopting the name of Christmas pottage or Christmas pudding. When the Victorians propelled it to the final course, they also added lucky charms designed to bring good luck and wealth to the lucky finders. They also put the pud into a pudding basin, and added a sprig of holly to bring us the dessert we celebrate with today.

62 *Age in years of a woman who found her image on the front of a Tesco's Christmas card in 2005, 47 years after it was taken*

CHRISTMAS IN PICTURES

When Margot invited George to see her in her Christmas stockings, this was not quite what he had expected.

QUOTE UNQUOTE

In December, the principal household duty lies in preparing for the creature comforts of those near and dear to us, so as to meet old Christmas with a happy face, a contented mind, and a full larder; and in stoning the plums, washing the currants, cutting the citron, beating the eggs, and mixing the pudding, a housewife is not unworthily greeting the genial season of all good things.
Isabella Mary Mason Beeton, writing in *Mrs Beeton's Book of Household Management*, 1861

Year in the 20th century in which the Beatles first topped the Christmas charts, followed by number ones in 1964 and 1965 63

NATIVITY TRADITIONS OF THE WORLD: MALTA

The Nativity scene is beloved by Christians around the world, with many cultures and customs 'making it their own'...

Most people in Malta and the nearby Island of Gozo are Catholic and the tradition of the Nativity crib is very important. Churches and homes contain Nativity cribs called *presepju*, built by churchgoers. These cribs are decorated with figurines called *pasturi*, with some even containing mechanical components so that they move. Rich Italian noblemen brought the first cribs to Malta in the 17th century. They slowly became popular but were toned down from expensive imports to rough clay and plaster depictions. When cribs were thought of as old fashioned in the early 20th century, a priest called George Preca started a tradition of having a Christmas Eve procession with a life-size figure of the Baby Jesus carried at the head of it. The first procession took place in 1921 and the tradition continues today. It is also traditional in Malta to sow wheat, grain and canary seed on cotton wool in flat pans five weeks before Christmas. When shoots spring forth, they are used to decorate the crib or a statue of the Baby Jesus.

CHRISTMAS ON THE OS MAP

Avid explorers can celebrate Christmas by doing a tour of Britain by festive place names. They include Cold Christmas in Hertfordshire; Christmas Cross in Shropshire; Holly Green in Worcestershire; and Ivy Tree in Cumbria. Father Christmas and his helpers also get a look in with Santa in Bedfordshire; Elf Hill in Aberdeenshire; Sleigh in Derbyshire; Reindeer in the Highlands; Dasher in Stirling; Comet in the Orkney Islands; Vixen in Devon; Cupid in Hertfordshire; and Sack in Wiltshire. In addition, it's year-round wintry days and evergreen decorations for Snow in Highland; Robin Hill in Staffordshire; Mistletoe Oak in Hertfordshire and Holly Bush in Wrexham. And if you still have some energy left you can make Christmas lists in Lists, North Yorkshire; write letters in Letters, Highland; prepare garlands in Garlands, Cumbria; put up stockings in Stocking, Hertfordshire; leave out carrots in Carrot, Angus; sing carols in Carrol, Highland; and eat turkey in Turkey, Somerset. You can even follow a star from Christmas Star in Fife to the North Pole in Norfolk and across to Bethlehem in Carmarthenshire. Just make sure you're back before midnight in Midnight, North Yorkshire, or trouble may be had.

 Percentage of Brits in the highest economic categories who expected to attend a Christmas church service, according to The Guardian *in 2006*

A CARROT FOR THE REINDEER?

Not so fast. The everyday diet of a reindeer does not usually include carrots, probably because they don't grow too well in the tundra. Instead you should tempt his four-chambered stomach with:

Arctic char
Birch leaves
Birds' eggs
Grass
Lemmings
Lichens (especially reindeer moss)
Mushrooms
Sedges
Willow leaves

THE ART OF THE ORNAMENT

Every year since 1988, The Tate has commissioned a leading contemporary artist to design its Christmas Tree. It is then exhibited in the Rotunda – the glass-domed hall and gallery of the Tate Britain. Twenty years on we can compare the trees across three decades, many symbolising issues that were important at the time:

1992 Craigie Aitchison

Aitchison created a tree decorated with animals influenced by early Italian art and religious themes, including a sheep inspired by a Byzantine mosaic, a donkey that references 'The Miracle of Spring', possibly painted by Giotto, and illuminated birds developed from an existing Christmas decoration owned by the artist. Animals play an important part in the Christmas story and the artist wanted to use them as decorations from an early stage. In his religious paintings, animals have always appeared as sympathetic onlookers, as in the design that he also created for the Tate Gallery Christmas card.

2002 Tracey Emin

No Christmas tree to be seen in the Tate this year. Instead, Emin chose to donate a tree to Lighthouse West London, a centre for people with and affected by HIV and AIDS. The Tate did receive a specially designed canvas and text installation inviting visitors to make a donation to the charity, in return for the opportunity to win an original artwork by Emin.

See the Christmas trees at
www.tate.org.uk/britain/exhibitions/christmastree

Year in the 20th century that the first song was broadcast from space when 65
Gemini 6 *astronauts sang 'Jingle Bells' on 16 December*

BEST-SELLING ALBUMS OF CHRISTMAS PAST – 1970S

From the British Library's *Pop Goes the Library* exhibition in association with The Official UK Charts Company, 26 July 2006 to 25 March 2007. More than 20% of albums are sold in December alone, many ending up in Christmas stockings.

Year	Album	Artist
1970	*Andy Williams' Greatest Hits*	Andy Williams
1971	*Electric Warrior*	T Rex
1972	*20 All Time Hits of the 50s*	Various Artists
1973	*Goodbye Yellow Brick Road*	Elton John
1974	*Elton John's Greatest Hits*	Elton John
1975	*A Night at the Opera*	Queen
1976	*20 Golden Greats*	Glen Campbell
1977	*Disco Fever*	Various Artists
1978	*Grease*	Original Soundtrack
1979	*Rod Stewart – Greatest Hits Vol 1*	Rod Stewart

THE THIRD DIMENSION

The first three-dimensional Nativity scene is attributed to St Francis of Assisi after his return to Italy from a voyage to Egypt and Acre in 1220. Some accounts state that he used statues or costumed people, but Francis' first biographer, Brother Tommaso da Celano (c1200 to c1260-1270), tells that he only used a straw-filled manger set between a real ox and donkey. The manger then acted as the altar for the Christmas Mass.

According to da Celano, Francis was merely emulating what he had seen elsewhere in previous years. This includes a request in 1223 to his friend and nobleman Giovanni Velitato to construct a Christmas Eve Nativity scene in a cave near the town of Greccio. Francis then preached at this scene.

The first Nativity manger or 'crib' of the modern kind was located in Prague in 1562, placed there by Jesuits or 'foot soldiers of Christ'.

66 *Percentage of UK consumers who shopped online over the Christmas period in 2007, according to the Office of National Statistics*

QUOTE UNQUOTE

Christmas is forced upon a reluctant and disgusted nation by the shopkeepers and the press; on its own merits it would wither and shrivel in the fiery breath of universal hatred.
George Bernard Shaw, British playwright

WHAT MARY DID NEXT

Mary the Mother of Jesus Christ is mentioned in the canonical Gospel accounts of the Bible several times. They include:

- In the Gospel of St Luke, the Angel Gabriel announces to Mary that she is to be the mother of the promised Messiah by conceiving him through the Holy Spirit
- Gabriel also tells Mary that Elizabeth, wife of Zachariah, is now miraculously pregnant; when she visits Elizabeth, she proclaims Mary as the mother of the Lord
- The canonical Gospels of St Mark, St John and the Letters of Paul do not explicitly mention the actual virgin birth of Jesus but the Gospel of Luke does tell us that Mary goes to Bethlehem with Joseph and gives birth to Jesus – because there is no place for him at the inn, she has to use a manger as a cradle
- After Jesus' birth, Mary flees with Joseph and her baby to Egypt to escape the wrath of Herod, and then goes back to the land of Israel to settle in Nazareth
- Along with Joseph, Mary is present when Jesus is found among the teachers in the temple, following his split from his parents after the Passover celebration in Jerusalem
- Many assume Mary is widowed after the Passover celebration when Jesus is about 12 years old, as Joseph is not mentioned again
- Mary is present when Jesus turns water into wine at the marriage in Cana
- The canonical Bible also tells us that Mary is present with Jesus' brothers, James, Joseph, Simon and Judas, which leads us to believe that she was not a perpetual virgin
- The canonical Bible tells us that Mary is present at the crucifixion
- In Acts 1:12-26, she is then present after the Ascension of Jesus, at the election of Mattias to the vacancy left by Judas in the group known as the 12 Apostles
- From this point Mary disappears from Biblical accounts, although some Christian groups believe that she is again portrayed as the heavenly Woman of Revelation in the Book of Revelation 12:1

THE ART OF THE ORNAMENT

Every year since 1988 The Tate has commissioned a leading contemporary artist to design its Christmas Tree. It is then exhibited in the Rotunda – the glass-domed hall and gallery of the Tate Britain. Twenty years on we can compare the trees across three decades, many symbolising issues that were important at the time:

1997 Michael Landy

Landy came up with an installation designed to comment on the physical residue of Christmas, seasonal gift giving and festivities. A large bin was filled with empty bottles, drink cans, used Christmas paper, broken decorations, the packaging from toys, gifts and food products, and dead, broken Christmas trees. This drew attention to the conspicuous consumption that so often surrounds the festive season.

2007 Fiona Banner

Entitled 'Peace on Earth', Banner took a 30ft-high traditional Nordic tree and decorated it with 123 handmade models of all the world's fighter planes that were in service at the time. The collection formed an A to Z of military aeroplanes but bore no markings of nationality. The tree was the largest of any installed in the Tate so far and the amount of research taken to find out about the planes and produce the kits was similarly huge. When assembling the collection, the artist also realised how many of the models had been named after birds, including the Harrier jump jets, the Albatross, Hawk, Falcon and Eagle fighters, and like birds, these symbols of war crouched among the branches.

See the Christmas trees at
www.tate.org.uk/britain/exhibitions/christmastree

A CARNIVOROUS CHRISTMAS IN CANADA

In a bid for new programming in 1986, the Canadian Broadcasting Company asked Canadian director David Cronenberg to fill the seasonal gap. Hot off his success with *The Fly* he proceeded with a 90-minute vision of surreal terror with a soundtrack of Neil Young, where Santa makes an emergency landing in the Northwest Territories and is exposed to a previously unknown virus after being attacked by a violent moose. Santa grows a vicious mouth in his belly and gets a lustful hunger for human flesh, which he sates by eating Canadian celebrities Bryan Adams, Dan Aykroyd and Gordie Howe.

 Year in the 20th century when the Beatles released the first Christmas fan club disc to be recorded separately

THE ANGEL GABRIEL APPEARS TO MARY

From Luke 1:26-27, in New Testament of the Bible:

'In the sixth month, the angel Gabriel was sent from God to a town of Galilee called Nazareth, to a virgin betrothed to a man named Joseph, of the house of David, and the virgin's name was Mary.'

TALES OF CHRISTMAS PAST

From Stave 1: 'Marley's Ghost'

Once upon a time -- of all the good days in the year, on Christmas Eve -- old Scrooge sat busy in his counting-house.

It was cold, bleak, biting weather: foggy withal: and he could hear the people in the court outside go wheezing up and down, beating their hands upon their breasts, and stamping their feet upon the pavement stones to warm them.

The city clocks had only just gone three, but it was quite dark already -- it had not been light all day: and candles were flaring in the windows of the neighbouring offices, like ruddy smears upon the palpable brown air.

The fog came pouring in at every chink and keyhole, and was so dense without, that although the court was of the narrowest, the houses opposite were mere phantoms.

To see the dingy cloud come drooping down, obscuring everything, one might have thought that Nature lived hard by, and was brewing on a large scale.

The door of Scrooge's counting-house was open that he might keep his eye upon his clerk, who in a dismal little cell beyond, a sort of tank, was copying letters.

Scrooge had a very small fire, but the clerk's fire was so very much smaller that it looked like one coal.

But he couldn't replenish it, for Scrooge kept the coal-box in his own room; and so surely as the clerk came in with the shovel, the master predicted that it would be necessary for them to part.

Wherefore the clerk put on his white comforter, and tried to warm himself at the candle; in which effort, not being a man of a strong imagination, he failed.

"A merry Christmas, uncle! God save you!" cried a cheerful voice. It was the voice of Scrooge's nephew, who came upon him so quickly that this was the first intimation he had of his approach.

"Bah!" said Scrooge, "Humbug!"

Charles Dickens
***A Christmas Carol*, 1843**

HOW TO... PLAY THE MISTLETOE GAME

You could just kiss under the mistletoe, but the Mistletoe Game, a Victorian parlour favourite, makes things even more fun (as long as your slippers are delicate enough to throw). Simply gather members of the party in a circle around a suspended piece of mistletoe. The first player then slides a slipper off and throws it, with the aim of trying to make it land under the mistletoe. If he or she fails, another tries. If he or she succeeds, there is a scramble in the direction of the man or lady towards which the slipper points. He or she must seize it and get away before being caught. Forfeits for all those caught out and kissing for any who end up beneath the match-making plant.

QUOTE UNQUOTE

The only blind person at Christmastime is he who has not Christmas in his heart.
Helen Keller, US writer and activist

CHOCOLATE LOG ANYONE?

The chocolate log has become a firm, but thankfully not woody, favourite at Christmas time, but where does the tradition come from? Indeed, its roots are planted firmly in the ancient festival of Yule, and stem from the associated custom of the Yule log. This was a large log, burned in the hearth as part of ancient festivities that happened around the time of the winter solstice. It has been suggested that the log burning was originally a custom among the Germanic peoples, in tribute to the god Thor who was also linked with oak trees. From the 12th century, in French and Italian history, a Yule log would be brought into houses with great ceremony. Then the master of the house would sprinkle it with oil, salt and mulled wine and say prayers. In some cases, the young ladies of the house would light the log with splinters from the preceding year, as was said that these splinters could protect the house from lightning and other malevolent forces. Some time in the late 18th century, the Yule log became a traditional French Christmas dessert called bûche de Noël. Its original form was as a large, rectangular yellow cake, spread with frosting and rolled up so that the cut end resembled the rings of the 'log'. In a bid to make the sweet log even more tree-like, a coating of chocolate or coffee icing was applied, along with candy holly leaves and roses, hence the 'chocolate log' of today.

 Year in the 16th century in which the earliest known reference to a Christmas tree was made, in a German pamphlet

CHRISTMAS CRACKERS

The ones you wish you'd never pulled...

JOKE: How many elves does it take to change a light bulb?

Answer on page 153

THE NATIVITY: JOSEPH

Some things you may or may not know about principal characters in the Nativity:

- Joseph is known from the New Testament of the Bible as the husband of the Virgin Mary
- According to Christian traditions Joseph is not the biological father of Jesus but acted as his foster or adoptive father
- In the Roman Catholic, Eastern Orthodox and Anglican churches, Joseph is venerated as a saint
- The canonical Gospels do not give the date or place of Joseph's birth or death but they do tell us that he lived at times in Nazareth in Galilee, stayed for a couple of years in Bethlehem in Judea and was forced into exile in Egypt
- Joseph's profession is described in the Gospels as a skilled craftsman – taken directly from the Greek – but Christian tradition has him as a worker of wood or carpenter
- Joseph never speaks a single word in the four canonical Gospel accounts
- There is some Gospel evidence that Joseph was a widower when he met Mary, with children from an earlier marriage
- Apocryphal sources elaborate on the account of Joseph with some putting him as much older than Mary and others describing Jesus as working side by side with Joseph in his carpenter's shop in Nazareth
- In pre-18th-century art and literature Joseph is often depicted as older, and with a beard in keeping with Jewish custom and his older years
- Joseph is often shown asleep
- In Roman Catholic tradition, Joseph is the patron saint of workers and has several feast days; St Joseph's Day is 19 March
- In the canonical Gospel accounts, the events narrated involving Joseph's presence include Joseph's relationship to Mary, a series of dreams and visitations by angels that tell him about Jesus and where to go at various points during his life, a visit by the shepherds after Jesus' birth and a visit to the temple in Jerusalem with his family

Length in minutes of the TV hit show Doctor Who Christmas Special *in 2007* 71

WHO IS SANTA CLAUS?

Santa Claus comes in many guises around the world and over time – such as St Nicholas and Father Christmas – that his origin is much disputed. Many believe the modern personification of him in red fur-trimmed robes with a big beard and jolly laugh stems from a Coca-Cola advert in 1931. These adverts, drawn by Haddon Sundblom, ran for 30 years and established Santa as an icon of contemporary culture.

But in fact this image of him began with a series of annual illustrations for *Harper's Weekly* by political cartoonist Thomas Nast, beginning in 1931. He took his inspiration from Clement Clarke Moore's popular poem 'A Visit from St Nicholas' penned in 1823, now better known as 'The Night Before Christmas'. Previous to this, US writer Washington Irving portrayed St Nicholas as a jolly laughing figure in his book *Knickerbocker's History of New York*, published on St Nicholas Day in 1809. Thomas Nast also based his cartoons on this work.

The shift of name from St Nicholas to the US-adopted Santa Claus is actually a natural phonetic alteration from the German *Sankt Niklaus* and Dutch *Sinterklaas*. Both these names come from the original 'St Nicholas', a 4th-century Greek bishop of Myra (now in Turkey). St Nicholas was famous for his generous gifts to the poor.

For this reason, St Nicholas is still portrayed as a bearded bishop in canonical robes in some parts of Europe. Since his relics were taken to Italy in 1087, and used as a magnet for pilgrims from around the world, St Nicholas has become the patron saint of many things, including children. In this way he draws a parallel with the modern Santa Claus.

Further theories say that Santa is based on Odin, a god of pre-Christian Germanic tribes who wore a big beard and cloak and carried a staff. He was said to ride an eight-legged horse called Sleipnir that could leap great distances – like Santa's reindeer.

Under the name of Father Christmas, the jolly figure we know and love is said to emerge in the early 17th century, when Christians under puritan criticism felt they needed a symbolic figurehead to protect their feast from being abolished. 'Christmas' appears in Ben Jonson's *Christmas, His Masque* in 1616 wearing a long beard, doublet, high crowned hat and crossed garters. He then appears in Thomas Nabbes' *The Springs Glorie* as 'an old reverend gentleman in furred gown and cap'. This image typified the spirit of good cheer at Christmas and was later reflected in Charles Dickens' Ghost of Christmas Past in *A Christmas Carol*.

Although Father Christmas was not traditionally known as a gift-bringer, nor associated with children, his image was merged with Santa Claus in the Victorian era. The idea of Father Christmas and Santa Claus as one figure continues today.

 Height in inches of a gold revolving fibre-optic Christmas tree on Amazon UK in 2008

CHRISTMAS IN PICTURES

As Lady Asquith wearily signed her 300th Christmas card, she wondered if it was time to teach the servants to write.

TALES OF CHRISTMAS PAST

Christmas Dinner

When the cloth was removed, the butler brought in a huge silver vessel of rare and curious workmanship, which he placed before the squire. Its appearance was hailed with acclamation; being the Wassail Bowl, so renowned in Christmas festivity. The contents had been prepared by the squire himself; for it was a beverage in the skilful mixture of which he particularly prided himself: alleging that it was too abstruse and complex for the comprehension of an ordinary servant. It was a potation, indeed, that might well make the heart of a toper leap within him; being composed of the richest and raciest wines, highly spiced and sweetened, with roasted apples bobbing about the surface.

The old gentleman's whole countenance beamed with a serene look of indwelling delight, as he stirred this mighty bowl. Having raised it to his lips, with a hearty wish of a merry Christmas to all present, he sent it brimming round the board, for every one to follow his example, according to the primitive style; pronouncing it "the ancient fountain of good feeling, where all hearts met together."

Washington Irving, *Old Christmas: from the sketch-book of Washington Irving*, 1886

Age in years of the soul star James Brown, when he died on Christmas Day in 2006 73

TALES OF CHRISTMAS PAST

There was more dancing, followed by games, in which Aunt Plumy shone pre-eminent, for the supper was off her mind and she could enjoy herself. There were shouts of merriment as the blithe old lady twirled the platter, hunted the squirrel, and went to Jerusalem like a girl of sixteen; her cap in a ruinous condition, and every seam of the purple dress straining like sails in a gale. It was great fun, but at midnight it came to an end, and the young folks, still bubbling over with innocent jollity, went jingling away along the snowy hills, unanimously pronouncing Mrs. Basset's party the best of the season.

"Never had such a good time in my life!" exclaimed Sophie, as the family stood together in the kitchen where the candles among the wreaths were going out, and the floor was strewn with wrecks of past joy.

Louisa May Alcott, *A Country Christmas*, 1882

PASS ME A CRIB PIE

One ancient recipe for mince pies from 1615 includes in its ingredients: two rabbits, two pigeons, a hare, a pheasant, a capon, the livers of all these animals, eggs, pickled mushrooms and dried fruit and spices. This is a far cry from the mince pies we eat today, which include a sweet 'mincemeat' of dried fruit, spices and alcohol but minus all the meat. Back in the day, a mince pie was also a huge affair, sometimes weighing as much as 100kg and held together with iron clamps. The pastry was either puft past (puff pastry) or short past (short pastry) and the shape tended to be oblong or square. Some say this was to mimic the shape of Christ's crib, with some pies having a pastry figure of a baby on top. This also gave them the name 'crib pies'. Then Oliver Cromwell came along and banned the huge but humble mince pie along with everything else to do with Christmas. When the Christmas ban was lifted and mince pies made a comeback, they were somewhat smaller and a custom grew where they were handed out to visitors over the festive period. This also earned them the title 'wayfarers' pies'. Today children like to leave a mince pie out for Santa in case he is hungry on his travels. One old saying goes that it is lucky to eat 12 pies in 12 different houses – in which case Santa, who visits children all over the world, should be a very lucky man indeed.

 Year in the 20th century that Cyclone Tracy devastated the Australian city of Darwin on Christmas Eve

THE ASSASSINATION OF ST NICK

In 1939, a Christmas Eve rendition of *A Christmas Carol* on Radio Columbia was hijacked by a 20-something Orson Welles who instead ran a hoax newscast that alleged that Santa's workshop in the North Pole had been overrun in a *blitzkrieg* by Finnish proxies of the Nazi German government. His hoax was a seasonal allegory about the spread of Fascism in Europe and was so convincing that tens of thousands of New York City children ran to Macy's Department Store on 34th street in New York to sing Christmas carols and weep for Santa's demise. It took New York mayor Fiorello LaGuardia to dress up as Santa and appear before them to stop their tears.

QUOTE UNQUOTE

Christmas at my house is always at least six or seven times more pleasant than anywhere else. We start drinking early. And while everyone else is seeing only one Santa Claus, we'll be seeing six or seven.
WC Fields, US actor

HAVE YOURSELF A SWINGING CHRISTMAS

Some 1970s Christmas albums, singles and bootlegs from www.mistletunes.com...

River .... Joni Mitchell
Ding Dong Ding Dong .... George Harrison
Merry Christmas (War is Over) .... John Lennon, Yoko Ono and the Plastic Ono Band
Wonderful Christmastime .... Paul McCartney
Jesus Christ .... Big Star
Christmas Day .... Squeeze
Child's Christmas in Wales .... John Cale
Step into Christmas .... Elton John
I Wish it Could be Christmas Every Day .... Wizzard
Merry Christmas Everybody .... Slade
Peace on Earth/The Little Drummer Boy .... Bing Crosby and David Bowie
I Believe in Father Christmas .... Greg Lake
Father Christmas .... The Kinks
Run Rudolph Run .... Keith Richards

WHITE CHRISTMAS… IN 60 SECONDS

A brief synopsis of the hit 1954 film White Christmas, *so that you can get your fix of snowy schmaltz at any time of year…*

The film centres on US army buddies Captain Bob Wallace (Bing Crosby), a Broadway entertainer, and Private Phil Davis (Danny Kaye), a would-be entertainer, during World War II. It's Christmas Eve 1944, somewhere in Europe, and Bob has enlisted Phil's help to put on a show for their fellow men. They sing 'White Christmas' for the first time. The two join forces as entertainers after the war and make it big in nightclubs, on the radio and on Broadway, and eventually become producers. Their first big hit is the New York musical *Playing Around*. Two years later the show makes its way to Florida where they receive a letter from a mess sergeant they knew in the war. He asks them to audition his sisters, Betty (Rosemary Clooney) and Judy (Vera-Ellen) Haynes. Bob and Phil go to a club to hear the girls sing, but the audition takes an unexpected twist when the club owner reports that the sheriff is backstage ready to arrest them. Betty and Judy's landlord has accused them of burning his lodgings with a cigarette and skipping rent. The club owner says he can arrest them when the show is over. Bob and Phil trick the sheriff and landlord into thinking the girls are still singing – in fact it is the men in disguise. The girls are well on their way to the train, with tickets given to them by Bob and Phil. The foursome end up travelling to Vermont together, where the girls want to go for Christmas because there will be snow. Bob and Phil discover that the Columbia Inn in Vermont is run by their former commanding officer, Major General Tom Waverley. They find out it is about to go bankrupt because of a lack of snow and therefore lack of visitors. What to do? Bring *Playing Around* and the entire Broadway cast up there and add Betty and Judy to the show. In an effort to make the show even more successful Bob calls Ed Harrison, an old army friend and host of a TV variety show. They put *Playing Around* on air, generating lots of free advertising for Bob and Phil. When Betty hears this, she thinks it is being done for the wrong reasons and leaves town. But all is set right when Betty sees Bob's pitch on the *Ed Harrison Show*, asking all the veterans of the 151st Division to come to Pine Tree, Vermont, on Christmas Eve. She returns to Pine Tree just in time for the show. When the general enters the Columbia Inn, he is greeted by his former division singing, 'We'll Follow the Old Man'. Moments later, snow is falling. Bob and Betty declare their love. Phil and Judy declare their love. The background set is removed to show snow falling everywhere. Everyone raises their glasses and sings the classic finale of the film.

76 *Year in the 20th century that snow fell on Christmas Day, the second of only two such occurrences recorded by the Met office that century*

CHRISTMAS CRACKERS

The ones you wish you'd never pulled...

JOKE: Santa rides in a sleigh. What do elves ride in?

Answer on page 153

CHRISTMAS IN PICTURES

The Saturnalia party was deemed a huge success, becoming more debauched by the hour. Christmas could wait.

CHRISTMAS DINNER IN... THE NETHERLANDS

On Christmas Day in the Netherlands you could be tucking into:

A *gourmet* (evening-long event where small groups cook together around little frying pans to create shared portions, thought to have originated in the former Dutch colony of Indonesia) consisting of:

- Finely chopped vegetables
- Meat
- Fish
- Prawns
- Salad
- Fruit
- Sauces

Or

- Roast beef
- Duck
- Rabbit
- Pheasant
- Roasted or glazed ham
- Vegetables
- Potatoes
- Salad

QUOTE UNQUOTE

Unless we make Christmas an occasion to share our blessings, all the snow in Alaska won't make it 'white'.
Bing Crosby, US singer and actor

SMS CHRISTMAS

It seems every generation finds a new way to wish their friends and family a happy Christmas. From plum puddings to mince pies to door wreaths and Christmas cards, we arrived in 1992 at the short message service (SMS) or text message. Sent on 3 December 1992 from Neil Papworth of Sema Group, on a personal computer, to Richard Jarvis of Vodaphone, using an Orbitel 901 handset, the text of the first commercial SMS message read 'Merry Christmas' – it was sent and arrived a full 22 days before the festive day had even arrived.

 Number of gifts often, and wrongly, thought to be given in the song 'The Twelve Days of Christmas' – the correct answer is 364

SPOT THE SOLSTICE

Many people now refer to the solstice – be it summer or winter – in relation to a whole day: one that signifies the longest day of the year and one that signifies the shortest day of the year. In fact, a solstice only happens for a moment. In the case of the winter solstice – celebrated in pre-Christian times around the same time as Christmas – this is at the instant when the sun's position in the sky is at its greatest angular distance on the other side of the equator from the person looking at it. Depending on how the calendar shifts, the winter solstice therefore occurs some time between 20-23 December each year in the Northern Hemisphere and between 20-23 June in the southern hemisphere. It takes place during either the shortest day or the longest night of the year. It does not occur, as many people think, during the darkest day or night, or the day with the earliest sunset or the latest sunrise. The word 'solstice' derives from the Latin word *sol* for 'sun' and the word *sistere* for 'to stand still'.

TALES OF CHRISTMAS PAST

The Christmas decorations were still up at Heritage. From the entrance gate all the way to the water slide, the place was festooned with Yule lights and other pagan symbols of the season–tinselled evergreens, holly wreaths, snowmen, candy canes. But no Santa Claus. His elves were there, stuffing stockings and wrapping presents, but Santa himself was nowhere to be found. When we walked into the hotel lobby, carollers were singing:

You'd better not frown
You'd better not cry
You'd better not pout,
I'm telling you why.
Jesus Christ is coming real soon.

And I thought Heritage was going to be dumb. But I'd only been there fifteen minutes and I was already confronted by enough serious theological questions to send St Thomas Aquinas back to Bible college. Did Santa die on the cross? Will he be resurrected at Macy's? Were Christ's disciples really elves? When the second coming happens, will Jesus bring toy trains?

While I puzzled over these mysteries, Dorothy went shopping.

PJ O'Rourke, from *Weekend Getaway: Heritage USA*, a story about a weekend at a born-again Christian resort and amusement park created by television evangelists Jim and Tammy Bakker, penned in January 1987 for *Holidays from Hell*, 1988

Percentage of children who felt that Christmas left them feeling happy, in a survey by BBC's Newsround *in 2006* 79

FESTIVE FLORA AND FAUNA: CARP

Ever heard of a Christmas carp? If you live in the Czech Republic you'd have a hard time not seeing the king of the ornamental pond – head to any town on Christmas Eve and you'll be greeted with tubs full of them. It's traditional to eat the carp for Christmas dinner, which follows a Christmas Eve fast. However, you can also choose a fish to set free in a river or lake. Either way, if you put a Christmas carp scale in your wallet or purse, the superstition is that you will have good fortune throughout the following year. Still the mind may be boggling: why the carp? It seems the Czechs have been making their fortunes from the golden fish for centuries, with the first written accounts of specially constructed carp fishponds dating back to the 11th century when monasteries maintained the ponds to provide food for Lent. In the 15th and 16th centuries, fishpond cultivation became big business, and led to the development of one of the biggest pond systems – the 45km-long Zlatá Stoka or Golden Drain followed by Rozmberk, a single pond covering a distance of 489ha. Today, fishermen harvest the fish from October to November just in time for the fishy feast.

MAKE ME A WASSAIL

Ingredients in a traditional wassail – a hot spiced punch associated with winter celebrations in northern Europe and connected with Twelfth Night and other Christmas holidays…

Mulled beer • Sugar • Ale
Ginger • Nutmeg • Cinnamon
Toast (as sops or soaking-up material)

SOME CHRISTMASTIDE AMUSEMENTS

In case you may run out of ideas to pass the time on Christmas Day and the rest of the festive holiday, Robert Burton lists a few popular 17th-century amusements in his 1621 book the *Anatomy of Melancholy*: 'The ordinary recreations which we have in winter are cards, tables and dice, shovelboard, chess-play, the philosopher's game, small trunks, billiards, music, masks, singing, dancing, Yule games, catches, purposes, questions; merry tales of errant knights, kings, queens, lovers, lords, ladies, giants, dwarfs, thieves, fairies, goblins, friars, witches, and the rest.' And maybe just a Chocolate Orange or two?

 Year in the 19th century that Woolworths first sold manufactured Christmas ornaments

WE THREE KINGS

Various texts since the Bible give additional details as to the names and clothing of the Magi – the 'three kings' who visited Jesus. Traditional names include:

Western churches	Caspar, Melchior and Balthasar
Ethiopia	Hor, Karsudan and Basanater
Armenia	Kagpha, Badadakharida and Badadilma
Syria	Larvandad, Gushnasaph and Hormisdas

SANTA'S LITTLE HELPERS: ZWARTE PIET

Luckily for Santa, delivering all the presents at Christmas isn't just up to him and his tribe of elves and reindeer – a whole troop of gift-givers are out and about spreading their joy. As long as you've been a good little girl or boy that is...

In the folklore of the Netherlands and Flanders, Zwarte Piet is a companion of St Nicholas. His name is translated as Black Peter or Pete and he was first depicted as a regular foreigner from southern Europe. Slowly his image was caricatured to merge with images of black servants and slaves. In Jan Schenkman's book *Saint Nicholas and his Servant*, published in 1845, he appears as a black slave wearing Asian-style clothes; in later editions he assumes more definite African origins while continuing to wear page costume. In this manner, he is seen as the personal servant of St Nicholas, possibly stemming from ancient myths that he travelled in the companionship of a devil, who later became his slave. St Nicholas was also said to come from Spain, which could explain the Moor-like appearance of his companion or slave. Zwarte Piet is often portrayed as a mischievous or even mean character: he was said to bring good children gifts and sweets, but if they had been bad he would chastise them with his switch, scoop them up and stuff them in his huge bag and spirit them away. Zwarte Piet traditionally makes his appearance a few weeks before St Nicholas Eve: 5 December in the Netherlands and 6 December in Flanders. A parade at this time indicates that he arrived in the country by steamboat from Spain. While this kind of parade still takes place today, Zwarte Piet is surrounded by controversy as many people think he promotes racism due to his blackened face. Plus children are often scared by his aggressive way of supposedly dealing with bad behaviour during the year.

Percentage of people who said that children should be encouraged to believe in Father Christmas, in a 2006 Populus poll 81

WRITE A CHRISTMAS POEM

Give the kids a fun Christmas task by getting them to write a poem, with each line starting with a letter from the word 'Christmas'. Or this could be a good one to play at the family Christmas party. Here's an example that we're sure you can better!

Come gather round now
Happy days are with us
Run through the snow
In joyful groups we go
Sing out carols of joy
Take glad tidings to friends
Make merry and make amends
Ask for peace on Earth
Say thanks for Christmas

TEN FACTS ABOUT POINSETTIAS

1. The Aztecs called the poinsettia *cuetlaxochitl*. They made a reddish purple dye from the bracts.
2. In nature, poinsettias are perennial flowering shrubs that can grow to ten feet tall.
3. The showy coloured parts of poinsettias that most people think are the flowers are actually coloured bracts (modified leaves).
4. The flowers or cyathia of the poinsettia are in the centre of the colourful bracts.
5. A fresh poinsettia is one on which little or no yellow pollen is showing on the flower clusters in the centre of the bracts. Plants that have shed their pollen will soon drop their colourful bracts.
6. Poinsettias represent over 85 per cent of the potted plant sales during the Christmas holiday season in the US.
7. The Paul Ecke Ranch in California grows over 80 per cent of poinsettias in the United States for the wholesale market.
8. There are over 100 varieties of poinsettias available.
9. Seventy-four per cent of Americans still prefer red poinsettias; eight per cent prefer white and six per cent pink.
10. Poinsettias are part of the *Euphorbiaceae* family. Many plants in this family ooze a milky sap that can give some people mild skin irritation.

From the University of Illinois Poinsettia Pages at www.urbanext.uiuc.edu/poinsettia

 Year in the 19th century that electric Christmas tree lights were first invented by Thomas Edison's assistant, Edward Johnson

HALLELUJAH

So goes the well-known chorus for one of George Frideric Handel's most famous compositions, the oratorio *Messiah* (commonly known as *The Messiah*), which, as the title suggests, alludes to the concept of Jesus as 'The Messiah' or 'anointed one'. Based on a libretto by Charles Jennens, it was composed in the summer of 1741 and premiered in Dublin on 13 April 1742. Although the word was conceived and first performed for the secular theatre during Lent, it has become common practice to sing out its verses during Advent, the preparatory period of the Christmas season. It is often performed in churches as well as concert halls and some ensembles present the entire work as a (very long) Christmas concert. If you catch one of these you will hear all three parts of the work, each addressing a specific event in the life of Christ. Part One is primarily concerned with the Advent and Christmas stories (often heard on their own during the festive season); Part Two details Christ's passion, resurrection, ascension and his message to the world; and Part Three is based upon the events chronicled in The Revelation to St John. In *Messiah*, Handel also uses what is referred to as text painting, where notes mimic the lyrics so that the word 'hill' becomes a rise and fall of sounds and the word 'low' gets a low note. Perhaps the most famous example of the technique is in 'Every valley shall be exalted', the tenor aria in the early section of Part I. Handy to know if you feel a little faint in an extra-long rendition and need something to focus on.

TALES OF CHRISTMAS PAST

From the 23 December 1835 entry:

...Late in the evening I went to Mr. Williams's house, where I passed the night. I found there a very large party of children, collected together for Christmas-day, and all sitting round a table at tea. I never saw a nicer or more merry group: and to think, that this was in the centre of the land of cannibalism, murder, and all atrocious crimes! The cordiality and happiness so plainly pictured in the faces of the little circle, appeared equally felt by the older persons of the mission.

Charles Darwin, *Journal of Researches into the geology and natural history of the various countries visited by HMS Beagle, under the command of Captain Fitzroy RN from 1832 to 1836* (commonly known as *'The Voyage of the Beagle'*), 1839

QUOTE UNQUOTE

When we were children we were grateful to those who filled our stockings at Christmas time. Why are we not grateful to God for filling our stockings with legs?
GK Chesterton, British writer

THE NATIVITY: JESUS

Some things you may or may not know about principal characters in the Nativity:

- The name Jesus is an Anglicisation of the Greek *Iēsous*, itself a Hellenisation of the Hebrew *Yehoshua*
- The title 'Christ' is derived from the Greek *Christós* meaning the 'Anointed One', which corresponds to the Hebrew-derived *Messiah*
- The main source of information about Jesus' life and teachings comes from the Gospels
- Christian views of Jesus centre on the belief that he is divine and the Messiah whose coming was prophesied in the Old Testament of the Bible; he is the Son of God and the second person in the Holy Trinity
- In Islam, Jesus is considered one of God's important prophets, a bringer of scripture, a worker of miracles and the Messiah; however they believe he is not divine and wasn't crucified but ascended bodily to heaven
- Judaism holds the idea of Jesus being God, or part of the Trinity, or a mediator to God, to be heresy; it also holds that Jesus is not the Messiah
- The actual year of Jesus' birth is disputed: the Gospels of St Matthew and St Luke place his birth under the reign of Herod the Great, who died in 4BC; scholars generally assume his birth to be between 6 and 4BC
- The common Western standard for numbering years is based on an early medieval attempt to count the years from Jesus' birth, which may explain the discrepancy of the term BC, meaning 'before Christ'
- According to St Matthew and St Luke, Jesus was born in Judea to Mary, a virgin, by a miracle of the Holy Spirit
- The Gospel of St Luke gives an account of the angel Gabriel visiting Mary to tell her that she was chosen to bear the Son of God. The Gospel of Luke also states that Mary and Joseph must use a manger in place of a crib due to a shortage of accommodation. Jesus is also described as being wrapped in bands of cloth

 Year in 20th century that Band Aid released the single 'Do They Know It's Christmas?'

THE ART OF THE ORNAMENT

Every year since 1988, The Tate has commissioned a leading contemporary artist to design its Christmas Tree. It is then exhibited in the Rotunda – the glass-domed hall and gallery of the Tate Britain. Twenty years on we can compare the trees across three decades, many symbolising issues that were important at the time:

1994 Cathy de Monchaux

Monchaux built a 20ft-high, 'invisible' Christmas tree, entirely encased in eight strips of canvas with blue velvet – suggesting the traditional colour of the Virgin Mary's robes in Renaissance iconography – appearing in the gaps in between. The edges of the strips were held together at intervals by intricate rusted metal clasps in the form of hands. From these hands came twisted cods that reached down to the ground and were grasped by similar hands set in eight amorphous lumps around the base of the tree. For the artist, the tree was a '20ft-high phallic object', its wrapping an illustration of Mary's sexual independence.

2004 Richard Wentworth

Wentworth brought visitors a traditional Norwegian spruce tree decorated with broken halves of plates and strings of dimmed domestic light bulbs. Test panels on the base of the tree described the histories of the tree's four elements: the light bulb, the plate, the Christmas tree and the plinth. Visitors were invited to interact with the tree by leaving digital presents – for example, photos, movies or texts – via the Christmas tree's Bluetooth antenna. The artist also auctioned the plates with proceeds going to the children's charity ArtWorks.

See the Christmas trees at
www.tate.org.uk/britain/exhibitions/christmastree

HOW TO... MAKE A DISH OF SNOW

It's a rare Christmas that's white these days, so here is a recipe from A Book of Cookerie, *1594, to help you make a dish of snow.*

TAKE a pottle of sweet thick Cream, and the white of eyght Egs, and beate them altogether, with a spoone, then put them into your cream with a dishfull of Rosewater, and a dishful of Sugar withal, then take a sticke and make it clene, and then cut it in the end foursquare, and therewith beat all the aforesaid things together, and ever ariseth take it off, and put it in to a Cullender, this done, take a platter and sette an Apple in the midst of it, stick a thicke bush of Rosemary in the Apple. Then cast your Snow upon the Rosemary and fill your platter therewith.

Length in miles of gift wrap used on Amazon UK's customer orders over the Christmas period in 2007 85

WHOSE CAROL IS IT ANYWAY?

Some popular Christmas carols and where they are believed to have come from, according to www.carols.org.uk:

'Away in a Manger'
Often the first carol that children are taught. This carol was originally published in 1885 in a Lutheran Sunday School book, creating the misconception that the lyrics were written by Martin Luther himself. The author of the lyrics is unknown but William J Kirkpatrick composed the music in 1895.

'Deck the Halls'
The music is believed to be Welsh in origin and reputed to have come from a 16th-century tune called *Nos Galan*. Mozart then used the tune for a violin and piano duet, while the lyrics are sometimes credited to one JP McCaskey. However, he only edited the *Franklin Square Song Collection* in which the lyrics were first published in 1881.

'Ding Dong Merrily on High'
The author of this carol is unknown but it is reputed to have originated in France in the 16th century. The lyrics were originally written in Latin as *Gloria in Excelsis Deo*. Children particularly enjoy singing this song due to the onomatopoeia of 'Ding Dong' and the breathless state achieved when singing 'Gloria'.

'God Rest Ye Merry Gentlemen'
This carol was first published in 1833 when it appeared in *Christmas Carols Ancient and Modern*, as collected by William B Sandys. The lyrics, as per the title, are traditional Old English and reputed to date back to the 15th century. It is believed that town watchmen sang this carol to gentry folk to help them make extra money at Christmas.

'Good King Wenceslas'
The words were written by John Mason Neale and published in 1853, while the music originated in Finland some 300 years earlier. The carol is unusual as there is no reference to the nativity. Instead it refers to Good King Wenceslas, martyred king of Bohemia in the 10th century, and a Catholic saint celebrated on 28 September.

'Hark the Herald Angels Sing'
This carol was written in 1739 by Charles Wesley, brother of John Wesley (the founder of the Methodist church). It was sung to a more sombre tune originally, but over 100 years later, it was adapted by William H Cummings to fit an 1840 cantata written by the composer Mendelssohn.

'O Christmas Tree'
A traditional German carol, the author of which is unknown. It must have originated around or post-19th century as this was when the tradition of decorating

 Percentage of people who said spending time with friends and family was the best thing about Christmas, according to think tank Theos in 2006

and displaying a Christmas tree became popular.

'O Come All Ye Faithful'
Originally written in Latin as *Adestes Fideles*, this carol was intended to be a hymn. The lyrics are attributed to John Wade and the music to John Reading, both Englishmen from the 18th century. The tune was first published, in Latin, in a collection called *Cantus Diversi* in 1751, with an English version in 1841.

'O Little Town of Bethlehem'
Rector Phillips Brooks of Philadelphia wrote the words in 1868, following a pilgrimage to the Holy Land. The lyrics follow his inspiration from the view of Bethlehem from the hills of Palestine, especially at nighttime; the music was added by Brooks' church organist Lewis Redner, who wrote it for the Sunday school children's choir.

'Once in Royal David's City'
It was one Mrs CF Alexander who wrote the words to this carol in the 19th century. Wife of the Bishop of Derry, she wrote many poems for children, chiefly on religious topics. HJ Gauntlett added the music later.

'Silent Night'
Originally a poem, written in 1818 by an Austrian priest called Joseph Mohr, the musical version of this carol is reputed to have come about on Christmas Eve in 1818 in a small Alpine village called Oberndorf. It is said that the organ at St Nicholas Church broke down that night and that Franz Xavier, Mohr's friend, composed the music to his poem to fill the gap. He created a simple score, designed for guitar, in time for Midnight Mass.

'The First Noel'
Early printed versions of this carol use the title *The First Nowell* – 'nowell' stemming from the French word *noël* for Christmas. Although the origins of the carol are unknown, it is thought to be English and dating from the 16th century. It was first published as 'The First Noel' in 1833, as part of *Christmas Carols Ancient and Modern*, collected by William B Sandys.

'We Three Kings of Orient Are'
US in origin, this carol was written in 1857 by the Reverend John Henry Hopkins. He is reputed to have written it for the General Theological Seminary in New York City as part of their Christmas pageant. Many people don't realise that 'Orient' and 'Are' are two words, mistakenly singing it as 'Orientar'.

'While Shepherds Watched'
This carol dates back to 1703 and is written by Nicholas Brady and Nahum Tate, poet laureate during the reign of Queen Anne. Brady and Tate were the first people to paraphrase the psalms for singing in rhyme, which became distinctive of their work. The melody of the carol comes from George Frideric Handel's opera *Siroe*.

Year in the 19th century that a fishing schooner called Christmas Ship *tied up at the Clark Street Bridge in Chicago, and sold spruce trees*

RUDOLPH AND FRIENDS

The 1964 stop motion TV animation of Robert L May's poem 'Rudolph the Red-Nosed Reindeer' by Rankin/Bass is so popular that it is still being aired and adapted today. In the animation, Rudolph also acquires some friends. They include:

Sam the Snowman The narrator
Hermey the Misfit Elf Prefers studying dentistry to making toys
Clarice the Reindeer Accepts Rudolph's nose and helps him fly
Yukon Cornelius A peppermint prospector
Tall Elf Generally tall, thin and bespectacled
Head Elf Foreman of Santa's workshop
The Bumble Abominable Snow Monster of The North
Fireball A blond reindeer who befriends Rudolph

QUOTE UNQUOTE

Charlie Brown is a blockhead, but he did get a nice tree.
The character Lucy exhibiting a rare display of tenderness in response to Charlie Brown's Christmas tree in *A Charlie Brown Christmas*, 1965

MINE'S A SMOKING BISHOP

When Ebenezer Scrooge has a change of heart at the end of Charles Dickens' book *A Christmas Carol*, he proposes discussing Bob Cratchit's affairs over a 'Christmas bowl of smoking bishop'. A 'bishop' was a very popular drink of the time, helping to raise the temperature on a freezing day. In the book *Drinking with Dickens* by Cedric Dickens (grandson of the great novelist), the recipe includes five sweet oranges, one old-fashioned grapefruit, ¼lb of sugar (to taste), two bottles of cheap, strong red wine, one bottle of ruby port and some cloves. The oranges and grapefruit are then baked in the oven until pale brown, and then pricked with five cloves each, before being placed into a warmed earthenware bowl. Sugar is sprinkled and wine poured over the fruit. The concoction is then left in a warm place for a day, after which oranges and grapefruit are cut and squeezed into the wine and the whole lot poured through a sieve to strain. The port is then added and the mixture heated (but not boiled). The bishop should then be served 'smoking' (as in hot) in goblets that are suitable for the occasion.

 Number of days that children would have to wait for Christmas to come around each year on the planet Mercury, according to Science@NASA

CHRISTMAS IN PICTURES

As Colonel Pigott explained his views on the economy once more, Boris was beginning to regret not booking that Christmas break in Thailand.

CHRISTMAS CRACKERS

The ones you wish you'd never pulled...

JOKE: Did Rudolph go to a regular school?

Answer on page 153

NATIVITY TRADITIONS OF THE WORLD: SPAIN AND BASQUE COUNTRY

The Nativity scene is beloved by Christians around the world, with many cultures and customs 'making it their own'...

In some places such as Parets del Vallè, huge Nativity scenes are built with more than 800 figures. Meanwhile, in Catalonia and the Basque Country, there is also a figure called the *caganer*, translated as 'crapper' and showing a defecating man. Large public cribs often depict a disliked public figure as the *caganer*. See page 98 for more detail.

FESTIVE FUN AT THE FROST FAIR

From 1400 up to the 19th century, there were 24 winters during which the Thames was recorded to have frozen over in London. King Henry VIII is noted to have travelled from central London to Greenwich by sleigh in a previous winter of 1536. During the Great Frost of 1683-1684, the Thames was completely frozen for about two months and the ice was reported to have been about 28cm thick in places. And the first frost fair – a fair that took place on the ice – was recorded as having happened in 1608. In diarist John Evelyn's account of the famous frost fair of 1683-1684, 'Coaches plied from Westminster to the Temple, and from several other stairs to and fro, as in the streets, sleds, sliding with ice-skates, bull-baiting, horse and coach races, puppet plays and interludes, cooks, tippling and other lewd places, so that it seemed to be a bacchanalian triumph, or carnival on the water.' While frost fairs are depicted as having been great fun for all classes and often picture-postcard for a time, Londoners also had to deal with the severe cold, the halt to businesses that used the Thames as a commercial thoroughfare and the aftermath of the meltdown. However, the image of the frost fair is still one that adorns Christmas cards now, along with winters of deep snow, sleigh bells and ice.

QUOTE UNQUOTE

The Supreme Court has ruled that they cannot have a Nativity scene in Washington DC. This wasn't for any religious reasons. They couldn't find three wise men and a virgin.

Jay Leno, US TV presenter and comedian

THE ANGEL APPEARS TO JOSEPH

From Matthew 1:18-21, in the Bible:

'Now the birth of Jesus Christ took place in this way. When his mother Mary had been betrothed to Joseph, before they came together she was found to be with child of the Holy Spirit; and her husband Joseph, being a just man and unwilling to put her to shame, resolved to send her away. But as he considered this, behold, an angel of the Lord appeared to him in a dream, saying, 'Joseph, son of David, do not fear to take Mary your wife, for that which is conceived in her is of the Holy Spirit; she will bear a son, and you shall call his name Jesus, for he will save his people from their sins.'

 Height in metres of America's official national Christmas tree – a giant sequoia – located in King's Canyon National Park in California

MARY, ALSO KNOWN AS

Mary, the Mother of Jesus, has been given many titles through time, religion and culture. They include:

- The Blessed Virgin Mary
- The Blessed Virgin
- The Virgin Mary
- Our Lady
- Notre Dame
- Nusetra Señora
- Nossa Senhora
- Madonna
- Mother of God
- Queen of Hevin
- Reina Caeli
- Theotokos (meaning Godbearer)
- Deipara
- Mater Dei
- Queen Mother
- New Eve
- Star of the Sea
- Cause of Our Joy
- Panagia
- Mother of Mercy
- Our Lady of Loreto
- Our Lady of Guadalupe
- Our Lady of Mount Carmel
- St Mary
- Holy Mary
- La Virgen Morena (The brown-skinned Virgin)

LET THE BELLS RING OUT

In the famous carol they're jingling, in the poem *Ring Out, Wild Bells* by Lord Alfred Tennyson they ring out for the old and the new among other things. In the 1973 song by Wizzard they aid the rouse 'I Wish it Could be Christmas Everyday' with that enthusiastic last line 'Let the bells ring out for Christmas'. Yes, bells and Christmas have been going hand in hand (but not just hand bells, mind) for hundreds of years, but most especially those church bells. The first ones to go off usually signal the start of the Christmas Eve service, as in Anglican and Catholic churches, the church day starts after sunset, so any service after that is the first service of the day. In some churches, it is also traditional to ring the largest bell in the church four times in the hour before midnight and then at midnight all the bells are rung in celebration of the birth of Christ. In many churches there is also a Midnight Mass service, where people can come and worship the Nativity, sing carols and hear the bells in all their pealing glory. In Victorian times it was also very fashionable to go carol singing with small handbells that would play the tune of the carol. In some cases, there would only be bells and no singing: for some, a welcome reprise from out-of-tune revellers but for others, a clashing performance that would be left resonating in the ears for days.

Percentage of Australians who would be spreading Christmas cheer through the giving of gifts, according to a 2006 survey of 11,000 people 91

ONE FOR THE ROAD

Parents bored of Sindy, Barbie and cutesie soft toys could give their kids something a little different for Christmas in 2007, something that would introduce them to the harsh realities of animal life on the road. Designed by toy creator Adam Arber, Roadkill Toys included Roadkill Teddy – complete with plastic body bag to keep maggots out and an identity bag giving details of its demise, namely being run over by a milk float last Thursday near the Hanger Lane Gyratory system in London. Roadkill Teddy's innards and blood could be stuffed in and out of his body, allowing the owner to zip and unzip them at leisure. Its eyes goggle, its tongue lolls and a tyre print runs across its back. Apparently Arber got the idea from looking at his mother-in-law's dog, a mutt he branded as ugly but thought would make a great toy. He merged this with a friend's pictures of roadkill to come up with the final idea. For those who have £25 to spare, other characters include Grind the rabbit, Splodge the hedgehog, Pop the weasel, Fender the fox and Smudge the squirrel. You can find them, along with their obituaries, CVs and Death Certificates, at www.roadkilltoys.com.

TALES OF CHRISTMAS PAST

Charley sighed. It was all strange to him, strange, morbid and disturbing. He did not know what to make of it. He felt more than ever ill-at-ease with that alien woman with her crazy fancies; and yet she looked ordinary enough, a prettyish little thing, not very well dressed; a typist or a girl in the post-office. Just then, at the Terry-Masons', they would probably have started dancing; they would be wearing the paper caps they'd got out of the crackers at dinner. Some of the chaps would be a bit tight, but hang it all, on Christmas Day no one could mind. There'd have been a lot of kissing under the mistletoe, a lot of fun, a lot of ragging, a lot of laughter; they were all having a grand time. It seemed very far away, but thank God, it was there, normal, decent, sane and real; this was a nightmare. A nightmare? He wondered if there was anything in what she said, this woman with her tragic history and her miserable life, that God had died when he created the wide world; and was he lying dead on some vast mountain range on a dead star or was he absorbed into the universe he had caused to be? It was rather funny, if you came to think of it, Lady Terry-Mason rounding up all of the house party to go to church on Christmas morning. And his own father backing her up.

W Somerset Maugham,
***Christmas Holiday*, 1947**

 Year in the 20th century that the film The Muppet Christmas Carol *was released, starring Michael Caine and the Muppets*

CHRISTMAS CRACKERS

The ones you wish you'd never pulled...

JOKE: Why couldn't the skeleton go to the Christmas Party?

Answer on page 153

AROUND THE WORLD WITH ST JOSEPH

Within the Roman Catholic and other Christian traditions, Joseph is the patron saint of various countries, regions and cities around the world. They include:

Countries

Austria • Belgium • Bohemia
Canada • China • Croatia
Mexico • Korea • Peru • Vietnam

Regions

Carinthia • Sicily • Styria • Tyrol

Cities and diocese

Baton Rouge • Bemidji • Buffalo
Cheyenne • Florence • Haugesund
Louisville • Nashville • San Jose
Sioux • Turin

FESTIVE FLORA AND FAUNA: REINDEER

Reindeers first attached themselves to Christmas through Clement Clark Moore's popular poem 'A Visit From St Nicholas' (now known as ''Twas the Night Before Christmas'). Moore has Santa's sleigh being led by a team of flying reindeers called Dasher, Dancer, Prancer, Vixen, Comet, Cupid, Donder and Blitzen. He may have based his poem on animals connected with the Yuletide god Thor, namely his eight-legged steed Sleipnir and the two goats that pulled his chariot: Gnasher and Cracker. Whether this legend was known to one Robert L May or not is another matter. In 1939, May came up with the famous ditty 'Rudolph the Red-Nosed Reindeer'. The imagined tale of a misfit reindeer that comes good, it was written for the marketing department of the Chicago-based Wards store where he worked. His poem was an instant hit and 2.5 million copies of it went home with Wards' shoppers that Christmas. May then republished the poem as a children's book in 1946 and Rudolph's story has assumed legendary status ever since.

Number in years that it took for a Christmas card to arrive, after being posted to Oberlin, Kansas, in 1914 93

THE BIRTH OF BRIAN

Classic lines from the Nativity scene of the hit of Monty Python's satirical film *The Life of Brian*, about a man who is born at the same time as and next door to Jesus, with whom he lives a parallel life...

[The Nativity: in a stable in Bethlehem, a baby lies in a manger. His mother, Mandy, is startled by the noise as three camels arrive outside.]

Mandy: Aarrgh! Who are you?
Wise Man 1: We are three wise men.
Mandy: What?
Wise Man 2: We are three wise men.
Mandy: Well, what are you doing creeping around a cow shed at two o'clock in the morning? That doesn't sound very wise to me.
Wise Man 3: We are astrologers.
Wise Man 2: We have come from the East.
Mandy: Is this some kind of joke?
Wise Man 1: We wish to praise the infant.
Wise Man 2: We must pay homage to him.
Mandy: Homage? You're drunk, it's disgusting! Out! The lot, out! Bursting in here with tales about oriental fortunetellers. Come on. Out!
Wise Man 1: No, no, we must see him.
Mandy: Go and praise someone else's brat! Go on!
Wise Man 2: We were led by a star.
Mandy: Led by a bottle, more like. Get out!
Wise Man 3: We must see him. We have brought gifts.
Mandy: OUT!
Wise Men: Gold! Frankincense! Myrrh!
Mandy: Well, why didn't you say? He's over there... Sorry the place is a bit of a mess.
Mandy: So, you're astrologers, eh? Well, what is he then?
Wise Men: Hmm?
Mandy: What star sign is he?
Wise Man 1: Capricorn.
Mandy: Capricorn, eh? What are they like?
Wise Man 2: He is the son of God... our Messiah.
Wise Man 1: King of the Jews.
Mandy: And that's Capricorn, is it?
Wise Man 3: No, no – that's just him.
Mandy: Oh. I was going to say, otherwise there'd be a lot of them.

 Number of years that Chicago boasted an annual Christmas Tree Lighting Ceremony, in 2007

Lucy and Ethel noticed how much more willing Dora was to stand under the mistletoe after they put a generous slug of gin in her tea.

HOW TO... MAKE A STRIPED CANDLE

Adapted from Ida Childs Field's description in the 1937 book 1001 Christmas Facts and Fancies *by Alfred Carl Hottes*

1. Select red and green, perhaps, or blue and white wax if such fits in with your decorations
2. Melt the colours separately, as several tints are desirable
3. Use a bottle of an interesting, candle-like shape. A catsup bottle may be used
4. Place a funnel in the top. Suspend a string into the bottle by means of a stick resting on the rim of the funnel
5. Pour in your first layer of wax
6. Clear the sides of the bottle by heating with a hot cloth
7. Then set the bottle in cold water to harden the wax each time before pouring the next layer. Thus your layers will be distinct
8. Cool overnight and the next morning break the bottle and your candle is now ready to be set in perhaps a copper or brass bowl

CHRISTMAS DINNER IN... AUSTRIA

On Christmas Day in Austria, you could be tucking into:

- Fried carp
- *Sacher torte* (chocolate cake)
- Christmas cookies such as *lebkuchen* (similar to gingerbread)
- *Glühwein* (mulled wine)
- *Rumpunsch* (hot rum punch)
- Goose
- Ham
- Chocolate mousse
- Edible Christmas ornaments

QUOTE UNQUOTE

Christmas is coming, the geese are getting fat.
Please put a penny in the old man's hat.
If you haven't got a penny, a half penny will do.
If you haven't got a half penny, then God bless you.
Traditional English Christmas rhyme

NO TIME TO BE A BOAR

Christmas past was certainly no time to be a boar, with the ancient feast of Yuletide putting a sacrificial boar's head at the centre of the table. According to folklore, the boar was offered to the god Freyr in return for good favour during the coming year. In old Swedish art, a boar is also shown in depictions of Yule banquets, and in relation to St Stephen, who is celebrated on 26 December. Today, the leftovers of yesterday's boar feasts include the Christmas ham – often eaten on Christmas Eve – and in special Boar's Head Feasts where a procession carries a boar's head and sings carols. One of the most famous feasts takes place at The Queen's College, Oxford, and was recorded as happening as far back as 1868 by William Henry Husk in his *Songs of the Nativity Being Christmas Carols, Ancient and Modern*. Other feasting points include Hurstpierpoint College in Oxford (since 1849) and Stourbridge Old Edwardian Club (celebrated since 1911) in England; and Reed College in Portland, Christ Church Cathedral in Cincinnati (since 1940) and St John's Northwestern Military Academy in Wisconsin in the US.

96 *Percentage of Americans who celebrate Christmas according to a Fox News poll in 2004*

THE ART ANGEL GABRIEL

Some famous artistic renditions of the angel Gabriel include...

c.1575	El Greco	*The Annunciation*
1420/30	Masolino da Panicale	*Archangel Gabriel*
1421	Jacobello del Fiore	*Justice between the Archangels Gabriel and Michael*
c.1425	Robert Campin	*The Annunciation* (the Merode Altarpiece – Triptych)
1450	Agostino di Duccio	*The Angel Gabriel*
1475	Leonardo da Vinci	*The Annunciation*

GROW YOUR OWN BRUSSELS

The name Brussels sprouts (*Brassica oleracea*) comes from their early cultivation in Belgium as far back as AD1200, but today, there's nothing to stop you growing your own, as long as you have a little bit of garden or even a window box. Sprouts produce their crops from late October to early March so you should be able to grow some in time for Christmas Day, plus a hard frost improves their eating quality, making them extra tasty at this time of year. They grow well in almost any soil (although they prefer a firm, non-acidic one as the plants can be top heavy) and grow equally well in sun or partial shade, but somewhere that is free from strong winds to help prevent their leafy stalks from breaking or falling down. Planting to harvest time is around 32 weeks and you can expect 1kg of sprouts per plant. Follow advice from www.gardenaction.co.uk:

Sow

Take some sprout seeds and sow in mid-April in a seedbed outside or in containers filled with potting compost. The plants produce a better root system if you plant in one place and move them a month or so later. The seeds should be sown 1cm deep and at least 10cm apart. Germination should occur in about 10 days' time.

Harvest

Remove sprouts with a knife to avoid breakage of stems. Take the lowest sprouts first and work up the stem as required, as the lowest ones mature first. As the season progresses, remove any leaves towards the base that are turning yellow. When harvesting is complete, cut the stem into pieces and put on the compost heap.

DECODING THE CAGANER

In some parts of Catalonia and the Basque Country, an extra figure is inserted into the Nativity called the *caganer*, translated from the Catalan to mean 'crapper'. Originally the caganer was depicted as a Catalan peasant wearing a traditional hat called a *barretina* – a red stocking hat with a black band. The local Catholic Church tolerates the caganer, although some people find the need to come up with a good, solid reason as to why a defecating man is placed in a scene that is widely considered to be holy. These include:

- Prevailing tradition
- Perceived scatalogical humour
- Finding the caganer is a good game, especially for children
- The caganer is fertilising the earth
- The caganer represents the equality of all people
- So that it is more believable, taken literally and seriously

SCENES FROM THE NATIVITY

In 2003, the Church of the Nativity in Bethlehem made a decision to ban a number of top coalition leaders from entering their house of worship due to their 'aggressive war on Iraq'. The banned included US President George W Bush, US Defence Secretary Donald Rumsfeld, UK Prime Minister Tony Blair and UK Foreign Minister Jack Straw. According to the Nativity Church's parishioner Father Panaritius, the four were 'war criminals and children killers that will be banned from entering the church for ever!' However, the banning was not the same as an official church ban or excommunication, which requires supreme church power – the Church of the Nativity is only under the jurisdiction of the Greek Orthodox Church, of which none of the banned is a member. Four years later in 2007, Blair was back in Bethlehem speaking of peace and reconciliation and promoting Western tourism to holy sites in the area, including the very same church. On his visit, he was presented with a typical Nativity scene – carved from the root of an olive tree – by Palestinian minister of tourism, Khouloud Daibes. According to a report at the time by the *International Herald Tribune*, Blair stayed in a Bethlehem hotel that overlooked a painting by British pop artist Banksy. It showed a dove with an olive branch in its mouth. The dove wore a bulletproof vest and centred over its head was a red target, as if viewed through a rifle sight. Three scenes from the Nativity, and not a shepherd in sight...

 Year in the 19th century that the first Christmas stamp was issued, in Canada

QUOTE UNQUOTE

At Christmas play and make good cheer,
For Christmas comes but once a year.
Thomas Tusser, British poet and farmer,
in *The Farmer's Daily Diet*

POPULAR PANTOS

Classic Christmas pantomimes generally have nothing to do with Christmas at all but are based on traditional stories or fairytales. Here are a few firm favourites:

Aladdin (sometimes combined with
Ali Baba and the 40 Thieves)
Babes in the Wood
Beauty and the Beast
Cinderella
Dick Whittington
Goldilocks and the Three Bears
Jack and the Beanstalk
Mother Goose
Peter Pan
Puss in Boots
Sleeping Beauty
Snow White
The Wizard of Oz

HOW TO... ROAST CHESTNUTS

'Chestnuts roasting on an open fire' sang Nat King Cole in 1946, but that's not the only way to serve them. You can eat them raw or roast them by following these simple steps.

1) Take as many chestnuts as you can eat
2) Preheat an oven to 200°C
3) Peel outside skin (the green spiky one) of nut if required
4) Use a very sharp knife to cut a 2.5cm cross into one side of the inside skin (the shiny brown one) of each nut to allow steam to escape gently
5) Put nuts in a roasting tin and bake until the skins open and the insides are tender – this should take about 20-30 minutes
6) Peel and eat them right away, pulling away the skin and the pithy white bit to get to the sweet kernel

Number of years that the British leased the Australian territory of 99
Christmas Island to Lever's Pacific Plantations Limited in June, 1902

TALES OF CHRISTMAS PAST

'Peace upon earth!' was said.
We sing it,
And pay a million priests to bring it.
After two thousand years of mass
We've got as far as poison-gas.

Thomas Hardy, 'Christmas: 1924', a poem, written on the 10th anniversary of World War I

ALL ABOUT TWELFTH NIGHT

Today, Twelfth Night is most commonly referred to as the day on which Christmas decorations need to be taken down so as not to bring bad luck on the home. However, the *Oxford English Dictionary* defines Twelfth Night as 'The evening of the fifth of January, preceding Twelfth Day, the eve of the Epiphany, formerly the last day of the Christmas festivities and observed as a time of merrymaking.'

With some cultures exchanging gifts on Epiphany – the day when the wise men, three kings or Magi were supposed to visit Jesus – Twelfth Night therefore takes on a similar role to Christmas Eve. However, some do celebrate on the eve of 6 January, veering away from the old custom of treating sunset as the beginning of the next day.

Others still base their 12-day count from 21 December – the winter solstice – with 12 days representing the 12 signs of the zodiac and taking them up to the New Year. The 12 days were simply the last days of a winter festival that began with All Hallows Eve or Halloween.

A Twelfth Night custom that stems from this time is the eating of Twelfth Night Cake. This cake would contain a bean and a pea with whoever ate them becoming king and queen of the feast. Those with high standing would also become peasants and vice-versa, with the Lord of Misrule – as the role reversal was called – ending at midnight on Twelfth Night. At this time 'natural order' was restored.

The other common reference to Twelfth Night is Shakespeare's play of the same name. It was first shown at Middle Temple Gall during the Twelfth Night celebrations of 1602. Designed to be performed during this time, the play also incorporates the role-reversal theme, with Viola dressing as a man and the servant Malvolio imagining that he can become a nobleman. During Shakespeare's time, men would also play the female parts of the play, although this is less common in performances of *Twelfth Night* today.

100 *Estimated number in millions of red crabs that take part in the annual mass migration on the Australian territory of Christmas Island*

SANTA'S LITTLE HELPERS: NISSE AND JULNISSE

Luckily for Santa, delivering all the presents at Christmas isn't just up to him and his tribe of elves and reindeer – a whole troop of gift-givers are out and about spreading their joy. As long as you've been a good little girl or boy that is...

In the Scandinavian folklore of Denmark, Norway and Sweden, elves or gnomes were believed to live in homesteads and farms. Not unlike Smurfs in appearance, with red hats and cute faces, it was thought that these elves took care of a farmer's home and children, and protected them from misfortune, particularly at night when everyone was asleep. In Denmark and Norway, one of these mythical creatures is given the name called Nisse or Julnisse and is thought to appear for 12 days over the Christmas period. While he brings protection and good luck all year round, it is considered wise to pay homage to him at Christmas by placing a bowl of porridge or rice pudding out for him to eat at night. He is considered to be a mischievous elf by some, and if food is not set out for him, he may cause havoc in the home or void his protection. Not something to chance if you want to have a peaceful Yuletide.

CHRISTMAS CRACKERS

The ones you wish you'd never pulled...

JOKE: Who delivers cats' Christmas presents?

Answer on page 153

DEAR SANTA... (FOR ADULTS ONLY)

Santa is real, of course. But just in case your little one doesn't believe you, why not arrange for Santa to send him or her a festive letter himself. Simply log on to www.fatherchristmasletters.co.uk and give your child's name, address – it can be anywhere in the world – to erm, Santa. You could suggest what kind of things your child likes and what he or she wants to know. Santa will then write back a letter filled with Christmas joy and tidings for the small sum of £5.99 (all proceeds go towards maintaining his sleigh, grotto and band of merry elves, we're sure). Santa even signs his letters so that you can be sure your child is getting the real thing.

Number of Christmas songs in the 101 Christmas Songs Box Set, *including songs by The Beach Boys, Jethro Tull and Nat King Cole* 101

CAST IN WHITE

Introducing the cast and main crew of the 1954 film *White Christmas*:

Director .... Michael Curtiz
Producer........................... Robert Emmett Dolan
Written by .... Norman Krasna
Music by .... Irving Berlin

Bob Wallace .... Bing Crosby
Phil Davis.. Danny Kaye
Betty Haynes .... Rosemary Clooney
Judy Haynes..Vera-Ellen
Major General Thomas F Waverley .... Dean Jagger
Emma Allen .... Mary Wickes
Ed Harrison .... Johnny Grant

FEAST ON... MRS BEETON'S CHRISTMAS TURKEY

A noble dish is a turkey, roast or boiled. A Christmas dinner with the middle classes of this empire, would scarcely be a Christmas dinner without its turkey; and we can hardly imagine an object of greater envy than is presented by a respected portly pater-familias carving, at the season devoted to good cheer and genial charity, his own fat turkey, and carving it well. The only art consists, as in the carving of a goose, in getting from the breast as many fine slices as possible; and all must have remarked the very great difference in the large number of people whom a good carver will find slices for, and the comparatively few that a bad carver will succeed in serving. As we have stated in both the carving of a duck and goose, the carver should commence cutting slices close to the wing ... and then proceed upwards towards the ridge of the breastbone: this is not the usual plan, but, in practice will be found the best. The breast is the only part which is looked on as fine in a turkey, the legs being very seldom cut off and eaten at table: they are usually removed to the kitchen, where they are taken off, as here marked, to appear only in a form which seems to have a special attraction at a bachelor's supper-table – we mean devilled: served in this way, they are especially liked and relished.

A boiled turkey is carved in the same manner as when roasted.

Isabella Mary Mason Beeton,
***Mrs Beeton's Book of Household Management*, 1861**

 Run time in minutes of both Christmas in Rome – The English Concert Orchestra *(2007) and* Vatican Christmas Concert *(2002) DVDs*

IT'S A WONDERFUL LIFE

The classic Christmas film *It's a Wonderful Life* was nominated for five Academy Awards and in 2006 the American Film Institute nominated it as the 'Number one most inspiring movie'. The Academy Award nominations were:

Best Actor for James Stewart
Best Editing for William Hornbeck
Best Director for Frank Capra
Best Sound Recording for John Aalberg
Best Picture for Frank Capra

ST NICHOLAS AND FRIENDS

In many European traditions, St Nicholas is accompanied by a group of closely replated figures. Here are some of the most well-known...

Knecht Ruprecht (Farmhand Ruprecht)
Krampus
Krampusz
Klaubauf
Bartel
Pelzebock
Père Fouettard
Petznickel
Beltznickle
Schmutzli
Hanstrapp
Zwarte Piet (Black Peter)

I WENT TO THE FROST FAIR...

...and all I got was a printed piece of paper that said I had been there. This was, indeed, what many people came back from the Thames' great Frost Fair of 1814 with (along with cold feet, no doubt), having visited one of the impromptu printing presses placed there especially to commemorate the calamitous phenomenon. One example, printed on the river Thames on 4 February in the 54th year of the reign of King George the III. Anno Domini, 1814, read:

FROST FAIR
Amidst the Arts which on the THAMES appear,
To tell the wonders of this *icy* year,
PRINTING claims prior place, which at one view,
ERECTS a monument of THAT and YOU.

FM frequency of California 103fm radio, which aired only Christmas music from 27 November 2007 and throughout the festive period

DONKEY CROSS

The cross-like shape on the back of a donkey is linked by Christians to the crucifixion of Christ, or the mark left by carrying a heavily pregnant Mary to a safe place to give birth to Jesus. From these beliefs sprung a whole load of 19th-century myths, customs and superstitions including:

- Using the dark hairs from the donkey 'cross' as a charm to heal ailments such as toothache
- Passing a child three times under and over a donkey to cure whooping cough
- Mixing the hairs with bread and eaten to bring good health
- Passing on a medical complaint to a donkey by putting a lock of the patient's hair in the animal's feed
- Letting a black donkey run with mares in a field to help prevent the mares having miscarriages
- Cutting hair from the 'cross' and hanging it from a child's neck in a bag to prevent fits and convulsions

FESTIVE FLORA AND FAUNA: THE WREN

If you see a group of straw-covered men running through an Irish, Welsh or Manx town on Boxing Day with what looks to be a wren attached to a pole, don't be alarmed, they're just keeping the ancient tradition of Hunting the Wren alive. Usually associated with St Stephen's Day celebrations (also 26 December), there are many stories associated with this custom. Some say that the little bird betrayed Irish tribes by beating its wings on their battle shields when the Vikings came to invade. Another legend says that the wren betrayed St Stephen, the first Christian martyr, by chattering in a nearby bush and alerting his enemies to his hiding place – hence the tradition taking place on that date. For these two reasons, the wren was hunted down, sacrificed and paraded on a stick. However, some historians believe that the wren actually symbolised good luck: in ancient Greek mythology, the wren is the king of the birds and his annual killing symbolised the end of one year and the beginning of the next; pre-Christian pagan Druids were said to use its flight patterns to foretell the future; while those who captured one of its feathers, were said to be protected from witchcraft – and in the case of fishermen and sailors, from shipwrecks. Today, Hunting the Wren ceremonies are enjoying a revival, albeit with a mock wren, so that the poor little thing may live to whistle another day.

 Number in years since a more fierce snowstorm raged in the Midwest compared to the one that occurred over Christmas in 2004

QUOTE UNQUOTE

I do come home at Christmas. We all do, or we all should. We all come home, or ought to come home, for a short holiday – the longer, the better – from the great boarding school where we are forever working at our arithmetical slates, to take, and give a rest.
Charles Dickens, British author

THE NATIVITY: THE SHEPHERDS

Some things you may or may not know about principal characters in the Nativity:

- The canonical Gospel of St Luke states that an angel appeared to a group of shepherds, saying that Christ has been born in Bethlehem
- The Gospel of St Luke then states that a crowd of angels appear to the shepherds saying 'Hallelujah, peace on earth to men of good will' – the shepherds are spurred on by this to visit Jesus in his manger, before they return to their flocks
- The speech of the angels to the shepherds became the initial part of the 'Gloria in Excelsis Deo', a short hymn of praise to God that appears in traditional Christian Mass
- Other shepherds of note in the Bible include Abel, Abraham, Isaac, Jacob, Moses and David, so the fact that the shepherds are the first people to hear about the birth may pay homage to this
- The Bible states that the shepherds were in the fields with their flocks at night when Jesus was born. This is the only indication of the season in which Jesus was born as shepherds only slept with their flocks at night in the warmer months – from this many conclude that 25 December can therefore not be the date of Jesus' birth
- Some Jewish traditions believe that the sheep were in the fields all year round, and as the sheep were meant for temple sacrifices, then the shepherds were not of the ordinary kind
- The clothes of the shepherds who visit Jesus are not described. However some signature shepherd items are mentioned in the 23rd Psalm of the King James Bible that refers to 'The Lord is my shepherd' and 'Thy rod and Thy staff they comfort me' – from this we may get many typical nativity costumes
- The ultimate spiritual shepherd is Jesus Christ, the 'good shepherd' who 'lays down his life for his sheep' in the Gospel of St John 10:7-18

WE BESEECH YOU ST JOSEPH

Within the Roman Catholic and other Christian traditions, Joseph is the patron saint of various actions, trades and associations. Roman Catholics also believe he prays for certain things. They include:

Patron of the Universal Church
Unofficial patron against doubt and hesitation
Patron saint of fighting communism
Patron saint of a happy death
Patron saint of workers
Prays for families
Prays for fathers
Prays for expectant mothers
Prays for travellers
Prays for immigrants
Prays for house sellers and buyers
Prays for craftsmen
Prays for engineers

INNOCENTS' DAY

For those wishing to extend their Christmas celebrations, Innocents' Day on 28 December is a date now often overlooked. It commemorates the alleged 'Massacre of the Innocents' – all those children who were two years and under – by King Herod when he heard that the Magi were looking for the King of the Jews. The 'Massacre' was described in the Bible in the Gospel of Matthew, although many modern biographers of Herod don't regard it as an actual historical event. Myth, legend or fact, the event lives on in many works of literature and art, including Rubens' *Massacre of the Innocents* now held in the Art Gallery of Ontario in Toronto and in Albert Camus' novel *The Fall*, where the main character argues that Jesus died on the cross because he felt guilty for not dying with the other children of Bethlehem. The commemoration of the Massacre of the Innocents – considered by some Christians to be the first martyrs for Christ – is first recorded in AD485 and today is either referred to as Holy Innocents' Day, Childermas or Children's Mass. In Spain, some celebrate it by playing *inocentadas* or pranks on each other, a bit like the tricks played on April Fool's Day, while some Catholics observe a role reversal between children and adults – definitely worth knowing for kids who want to rule the roost over their elders for the day.

 The second Psalm number used on Cliff Richard's The Christmas Story, *a CD produced with The Choristers of Exeter Cathedral in 2007*

CHRISTMAS CRACKERS

The ones you wish you'd never pulled...

JOKE: What do reindeer hang on their Christmas trees?

Answer on page 153

PANTO SUPERSTITIONS AND TRADITIONS

From www.its-behind-you.com:

- The Fairy always enters from the right (Stage Right) and the Demon from the left (Stage Left). It has been said that, in older theatres, the stage trap through which the Demon rose was generally located on the left side of the stage.
- When speaking, the Pantomime Fairy should transfer her wand from her right hand to her left, to protect her heart from the Demon King.
- The last people to appear onstage in a Pantomime 'walk down' or finale are traditionally the Principal Boy and Girl, the idea being that they are just married.
- In the days of the Harlequinade, the Harlequin's coloured suit was of great significance. Yellow was for jealousy, red for anger, blue for his faithfulness to Columbine, and black for his power of invisibility. Harlequin would point to the colour on his costume, so that the audience knew his mood, or his transition into invisibility.
- Green has always been regarded as an unlucky colour on stage. This can cause problems if the pantomime happens to be Robin Hood, and his Merry Men are in Lincoln Green.
- It is very unlucky to have real flowers on stage, unless handed up to the leading lady at the curtain call.
- Tripping over in the wings, or on your first entrance is regarded as very lucky.
- Whistling in a dressing room is a bad omen. The person caught doing this is made to leave the room, turn around three times, knock and re-enter, usually uttering a curse.
- Clapping in the wings is regarded as very unlucky. In the days of Harlequin, the actor would clap his 'Slapstick' loudly, to indicate to the stage crew it was time to change the scenery. Pre-technology, clapping was only to be done by the stage manager.

REMEMBERING THE TSUNAMI

26 December 2004 was just another Boxing Day for many people around the world but in South Asia, Southeast Asia and Somalia, a series of tsunamis killed thousands of people and saw millions lose their livelihoods and homes. In the UK, the Disaster Emergency Committee (DEC) launched an immediate appeal to respond to this devastating natural disaster, raising £60 million within one week and £390 million by the end of the fundraising campaign in 2005. The funds provided emergency relief aid for temporary housing, clean water, food supplies and medical services and has helped to rebuild villages, schools and hospitals as well as fishing ports and factories. Many people are still affected by the disaster, having lost loved ones and their former habitats and communities, so this Christmas spare a thought or a prayer for them and others in similar situations around the world.

You can find out more about where the money has been spent and how tsunami victims are getting on at www.dec.org.uk. You can also find information on current appeals that may need your help.

QUOTE UNQUOTE

'Me – I am not an Englishman,' said Hercule Poirot. 'In my country, Christmas, it is for the children. The New Year, that is what we celebrate.'

Hercule Poirot, in the Agatha Christie novel *The Adventures of the Christmas Pudding*

I WORSHIP THEE WITH MY PRETZEL

A hot pretzel is the ideal snack on a cold winter morning or after a spot of festive ice-skating near Central Park in New York. But you can also celebrate the winter solstice by eating one. According to the 1937 book *1001 Christmas Facts and Fancies* by Alfred Carl Hottes, 'the old calendar sign of the winter solstice was a circle with a dot in the center'. This represented the wheel of the sun, and 'a symbolical cracker was made at this season, called a Bretzel or Pretzel'. Apparently, the original form was a circle of dough with a cross at the centre to represent the four seasons, while its present form is a variation caused by making the cracker out of one piece of dough.

108 *Episode number of* Martha Stewart's Crafts *that delves into Christmas crafts, including transforming household jars into snow globes*

CHRISTMAS DINNER IN... FINLAND

On Christmas Day in Finland you could be tucking into:

A *Joulupöytä* (Christmas table, similar to a Swedish *smörgåsbord*) of:

- Large ham
- Mustard
- Bread
- Lutefisk and gravlax (fish)
- *Laatikot* (casseroles with liver and raisins, or potatoes, or rice and carrots)
- *Glögi* (mulled wine)

BEST-SELLING ALBUMS OF CHRISTMAS PAST – 1980s

From the British Library's *Pop Goes the Library* exhibition in association with The Official UK Charts Company, 26 July 2006 to 25 March 2007. More than 20% of albums are sold in December alone, many ending up in Christmas stockings.

1980	*Super Trouper*	Abba
1981	*The Visitors*	Abba
1982	*The John Lennon Collection*	John Lennon
1983	*Now That's What I Call Music*	Various Artists
1984	*The Hits Album/The Hits Tape – 32 Original Hits*	Various Artists
1985	*Now – The Christmas Album*	Various Artists
1986	*Now That's What I Call Music 8*	Various Artists
1987	*Now That's What I Call Music 10*	Various Artists
1988	*Private Collection 1979-1988*	Cliff Richard
1989	*But Seriously*	Phil Collins

THE NUTCRACKER... IN 60 SECONDS

A brief synopsis of the classic ballet The Nutcracker, *so that you can get your fix of twirling toys at any time of year. The ballet is based on a story by ETA Hoffman called* The Nutcracker and the King of Mice, *later adapted by the French author Alexander Dumas pére. Following a 1981 commission from Ivan Vsevolozhsky, the director of the Imperial Theatres in Russia, the fairytale was then turned into a two-act, three-scene ballet by writer Marius Petipa and composer Pyotr Il'yich Tchaikovsky...*

The story begins on Christmas Eve at the very grand Stahlbaum house, where the family are hosting their annual Christmas party. The Christmas tree is particularly beautiful and the children are dancing and playing. Suddenly Herr Drosselmeyer arrives, a mysterious clock and toymaker who is always full of surprises. He draws the party's attention to two life-sized dolls that each take a turn to dance. The children then begin to open their presents. Clara receives a beautiful nutcracker that becomes the hit of the party. In a jealous rage, her brother Fritz grabs the nutcracker and breaks it. Drosselmeyer fixes it with a handkerchief that he draws magically from the air. When the party is finished, guests leave and everyone retires to bed. But Clara goes back downstairs to check on her poor nutcracker and falls asleep with him (the Nutcracker is personified as a male in this instance) in her arms. As the clock strikes midnight, Clara starts shrinking and the toys around the tree come to life. They include an army of mice led by the fierce Mouse King. The Nutcracker wakes up too and leads his army of toy soldiers into battle with the mice. But no match for the fierce Mouse King, the Nutcracker and his army are eventually captured. Clara saves the day by throwing her slipper at the Mouse King, hitting him on the head. He drops to the floor and the mice run away. The Nutcracker then turns into a prince and transports Clara to the Land of Snow and then the Land of Sweets, where Clara and the prince are greeted by the Sugar Plum Fairy. For their daring battle against the army of mice, the fairy rewards them with a round of character dances, not always in this order: the Spanish Dance (sometimes Chocolate), the Arabian Dance (sometimes Coffee), the Russian Dance (sometimes Candy Canes), the Chinese Dance (sometimes Tea), Mother Ginger and her Polichinelles (sometimes BonBons), The Reed Flute Dance (sometimes marzipan shepherds or Mirlitons) and the Waltz of Flowers. After the festivities, Clara wakes up under the Christmas tree with the Nutcracker still in her arms. In some versions, she rides off with the Nutcracker prince, thus giving the impression that the 'dream' actually happened. And then the curtain falls.

110 *Episode number of the* South Park *animation 'A South Park Christmas', introducing Mr Hankey, the Christmas Poo*

CHRISTMAS IN PICTURES

Despite her best efforts, Cook failed to convince Monsieur Roux of the delights of bread sauce.

MARY, A STARRING ROLE

For those seeking inspiration for their nativity costumes, Mary, the Mother of Christ, has been portrayed in several films, although not all descriptions could be said to be true. They include:

1943	Linda Darnell	*The Song of Bernadette*
1951	Angela Clarke	*The Miracle of Our Lady of Fatima*
1961	Siobhán McKenna	*King of Kings*
1977	Olivia Hussey	*Jesus of Nazareth*
1988	Verna Bloom	*The Last Temptation of Christ*
1999	Pernilla August	*Mary, Mother of Jesus*
2004	Maia Morgenstern	*The Passion of Christ*
2006	Keisha Castle-Hughes	*The Nativity Story*
2008	Penelope Wilton	*The Passion* (TV)

Number of miles in millions calculated by physicians Joel Potischman and Bruce Handy to be the distance travelled by Santa Claus each year

QUOTE UNQUOTE

Christmas is a time when people of all religions come together to worship Jesus Christ.
Bart Simpson, in *The Simpsons*

TALES OF CHRISTMAS PAST

After playing lady's-maid to the new-comer, and putting my cakes in the oven, and making the house and kitchen cheerful with great fires, befitting Christmas-eve, I prepared to sit down and amuse myself by singing carols, all alone; regardless of Joseph's affirmations that he considered the merry tunes I chose as next door to songs. He had retired to private prayer in his chamber, and Mr. and Mrs. Earnshaw were engaging Missy's attention by sundry gay trifles bought for her to present to the little Lintons, as an acknowledgment of their kindness. They had invited them to spend the morrow at Wuthering Heights, and the invitation had been accepted, on one condition: Mrs. Linton begged that her darlings might be kept carefully apart from that 'naughty swearing boy.'

Under these circumstances I remained solitary. I smelt the rich scent of the heating spices; and admired the shining kitchen utensils, the polished clock, decked in holly, the silver mugs ranged on a tray ready to be filled with mulled ale for supper; and above all, the speckless purity of my particular care—the scoured and well-swept floor. I gave due inward applause to every object, and then I remembered how old Earnshaw used to come in when all was tidied, and call me a cant lass, and slip a shilling into my hand as a Christmas-box; and from that I went on to think of his fondness for Heathcliff, and his dread lest he should suffer neglect after death had removed him: and that naturally led me to consider the poor lad's situation now, and from singing I changed my mind to crying. It struck me soon, however, there would be more sense in endeavouring to repair some of his wrongs than shedding tears over them: I got up and walked into the court to seek him. He was not far; I found him smoothing the glossy coat of the new pony in the stable, and feeding the other beasts, according to custom.

'Make haste, Heathcliff!' I said, 'the kitchen is so comfortable; and Joseph is up-stairs: make haste, and let me dress you smart before Miss Cathy comes out, and then you can sit together, with the whole hearth to yourselves, and have a long chatter till bedtime.'

He proceeded with his task, and never turned his head towards me.

Emily Brontë,
***Wuthering Heights*, 1850**

 Number of Christmas cards that Hyacinth Bouquet has at the start of the Keeping up Appearances *episode 'A Father Christmas Suit'*

THE ART OF THE ORNAMENT

Every year since 1988 The Tate has commissioned a leading contemporary artist to design its Christmas Tree. It is then exhibited in the Rotunda – the glass-domed hall and gallery of the Tate Britain. Twenty years on we can compare the trees across three decades, many symbolising issues that were important at the time:

1996 Julian Opie

Opie didn't want to settle for just one tree, but created a whole forest constructed out of a number of model trees. Opie had fabricated trees for his shows over the preceding year, so the theme was already present in his work. His highly stylised Christmas tees were constructed from two intersecting planes of wood, with a serrated outline to make them instantly recognisable as fir trees. Individually, the trees resembled oversize children's toys. As a group, they became more mysterious, drawing visitors into an interior space and evoking the idea of a forest.

2006 Sarah Lucas

Lucas decorated her tree with sculptures that took the form of baby angels made from wire and stretched tights. A chorus of fairies referred to figures from the classics such as Cupid, Eros and Venus, descending from above and multiplying over the tree. The artist used her tree to question the erotic overtones often associated with these mythical figures, through their use as decorations and matter-of-fact material quality.

See the Christmas trees at
www.tate.org.uk/britain/exhibitions/christmastree

NAME THE NATIVITY

Common names for the Nativity in other countries and cultures...

Italy	*Presepe* or *Presepio*
Portuguese	*Presépio*
Catalan	*Pessebre*
Spanish	*El Belén* and *Nacimiento*, *Portal* or *Pesebre*
Poland	*Szopka*
Croatian	*Jaslice*
Belarus	*Batleyka*
Philippines	*Belen*

Size in feet of the world's biggest ever snowman, built by residents of the state of Maine in America in 1999

WE'RE DREAMING OF A WHITE CHRISTMAS

Just some of the musicians and singers who have recorded or performed their own version of the classic festive song 'White Christmas':

Bing Crosby	1942, the first recording
Frank Sinatra	1944
Louis Armstrong	1952
Elvis Presley	1957
Johnny Mathis	1958
Dean Martin	1959
Peggy Lee	1960
Jerry Lee Lewis	1962
Andy Williams	1963
The Beach Boys	1964
Bob Marley	1965
Barbara Streisand	1967
Otis Reading	1968
Tammy Wynette	1970
Gloria Estefan	1993
Ringo Star	1999
The Flaming Lips	2000
The Moody Blues	2003
Girls Aloud	2005
Billy Idol	2006

FESTIVE FLORA AND FAUNA: THE HOLLY AND THE IVY

First published in 1710 and then in a collection of songs by folk aficionado Cecil Sharp in 1909, the rousing carol 'The Holly and the Ivy' was an immediate hit with the Victorians. But while the song goes that the holly's crown, flower, berry, prickle and bark symbolise the suffering of Christ, the holly and the ivy have long been intertwined, growing symbiotically in woodlands and then woven together in Yuletide crowns. In these crowns, the rigid and prickly holly was conceived of as being masculine, while the softer, tendril-like ivy was associated with the feminine. Ivy was also associated with Bacchus, the Roman god of wine, while holly featured prominently in the Romans' celebrations for Saturnalia (a festive precursor for Christmas). The tradition of decorating homes with holly and ivy for seasonal good luck continued for many years, and was eventually also adopted by the Church. The holly and the ivy, in both decorative and carol form, are still popular components of Christmas celebrations today.

114 *Number of companies who signed up to the 2006 Crisis Christmas Card Challenge, raising £807,850 to open doors for homeless people*

CHRISTMAS DINNER IN... AUSTRALIA

On Christmas Day in Australia, you could be tucking into:

- Cold meat (chicken, ham and turkey)
- Barbecued meat and fish
- Prawns
- White Christmas (a traditional dessert)
- Mangos
- Cherries

IT'S A WONDERFUL LIFE... IN 60 SECONDS

A brief synopsis of the 1946 film It's a Wonderful Life, *so that you can get your fix of Christmas classics at any time of year...*

Based on the short story *The Greatest Gift* by Phillip Van Doren Stern, *It's a Wonderful Life* takes place in the fictional town of Bedford Falls, shortly after World War II. It stars James Stewart as George Bailey, a man whose attempted suicide on Christmas Eve prompts his guardian angel Clarence Odbury to help him change his mind. He does this by showing him clips of his life, highlighting all the good he has done. This includes: saving the life of his younger brother Harry; saving another child's life; sacrificing his dreams to be an architect so that his brother can graduate; setting up home loans for the working poor by running the family business; marrying a wonderful woman called Mary who helps him save the townspeople of Bedford Falls from panic in the Great Depression; starting up an affordable housing project called Bailey Park; and raising a family. Despite all these things George is depressed and the final straw is when a nasty competitive businessman, Mr Potters, tries to dupe him out of money and drive the family business into the ground. To help drive home the 'wonderful life' message, Clarence shows George what life would have been like if he had never been born. Among other things: Bedford Falls would be called Pottersville, a slum city dominated by pawn shops and sleazy bars; Mary would be a spinster librarian; his widow mother would be running a boarding house; Harry would be dead and so would all the people he saved in the war. George finally sees the light and appeals to God to give him back his life. His wish is granted and he returns home with a new zest for life. In return the grateful townspeople have collected a huge amount of money to save his business. George finally realises what a wonderful life he has. The end.

THE MAKING OF CHRISTMAS DAY

25 December is internationally known as Christmas Day, the day on which Christians celebrate the birth of Jesus. But how did we come by this date?

In the biblical sense, Christmas Day refers to the birth of Christ, and also the start of a season of celebration that culminates with the Feast of Epiphany on 6 January. Although we now celebrate Christmas Day on 25 December, this is not considered to be Jesus' actual birthday. The date has come about through the amalgamation of Christian worship, pagan festivals and other ancient festivities.

Although it is not known exactly when 25 December became synonymous with Christ's birth, the earliest reference to the celebration of the Nativity on that day is found in the *Chronography of 354*, an illuminated manuscript compiled in Rome in 354.

Christmas Day, as a Christian celebration of this Nativity, then came to prominence after King Charlemagne – considered to be the 'Father of Europe' and a reviver of the arts, religion and culture through the medium of the Catholic faith, as well as Charles I of France, Germany and the Holy Roman Empire – was crowned on Christmas Day in 800. Some four centuries later, the remnants of Roman Saturnalian traditions were transferred to the Twelve Days of Christmas and Christmas became a public festival throughout the Middle Ages.

In part, Christmas Day was 'invented' by the early Church to entice pagan Romans to convert to Christianity without losing their own winter celebrations. The pre-Christian Romans already held a winter festival on 25 December, entitled *Dies Natalis Solis Invicti*, or 'the birthday of the undefeated sun'. Although introduced by Emperor Elagabalus (218-222), this festival was at the height of its popularity under Emperor Aurelian (270-275), who promoted it as an empire-wide holiday.

During the times of the Julian calendar (introduced by Julius Caesar in 45BC), 25 December was also considered to be the date of the winter solstice. Since the adoption of the Gregorian calendar, in 1752 for the British Empire, this now falls on 21-22 December.

A Scandinavian Pagan festival called Yule also merged with Christian celebrations. Yule was held in late December to early January.

As for the name 'Christmas', this originated as a contraction of 'Christ's mass'. Derived from the Middle English *Christemasse* and old English *Christes maesse*, this phrase was first recorded in 1038. These come from the Greek *Christos* and the Latin *missa*.

With Christmas still celebrated on 25 December today, it doesn't look as if things will change unless a new deity arrives to push it off its post – or we change the calendar again…

CHRISTMAS IN PICTURES

It was not long after their Christmas lunch that the Joneses' discovered the truth of the saying 'You are what you eat.'

TALES OF CHRISTMAS PAST

And the Grinch, with his Grinch-feet ice cold in the snow, stood puzzling and puzzling, how could it be so? It came without ribbons. It came without tags. It came without packages, boxes or bags. And he puzzled and puzzled 'till his puzzler was sore. Then the Grinch thought of something he hadn't before. What if Christmas, he thought, doesn't come from a store. What if Christmas, perhaps, means a little bit more.

Dr Seuss, *How the Grinch Stole Christmas*, 1957

Distance in miles rowed by the crew of La Mondiale *on 3 January, on a voyage across the Atlantic that began on 15 December 2007* 117

TAKE THE PARTY OUT OF CHRISTMAS

Not literally, of course as this is one of the best times to party. But if you have a quiet moment and are stuck for something to do – or maybe you want to stave off the boredom of Boxing Day – why not try making an anagram out of the phrase 'Happy Christmas'. It can be broken down to make lots of words that relate to this festive time, for example, 'party' and 'misty'. How many words can you find? Here's the phrase in capital letters to help get you started:

HAPPY CHRISTMAS

SANTA'S LITTLE HELPERS: DED MOROZ

Luckily for Santa, delivering all the presents at Christmas isn't just up to him and his tribe of elves and reindeer – a whole troop of gift-givers are out and about spreading their joy. As long as you've been a good little girl or boy that is...

Although Ded Moroz, 'Father Frost' or 'Grandfather Frost' has some roots in Russian folklore, his shift from frosty winter sprite to ornately robed Christmas gift-bringer took place in the late 1800s. After the Russian Revolution in 1917, the Bolsheviks began to wage a war against religion. This meant that the celebration of figures such as Ded Moroz was forbidden, along with the Nativity of Christ, St Nicholas, Kolyada (Father Christmas) and Babushka. The Christmas or New Year Tree was also banished, as this was imported from Germany, Russia's enemy during World War I. However, Stalin brought Ded Moroz back in 1935 and he made his first appearance in 1937 at the Palace of Unions. He is traditionally known as a tall gentlemanly figure, in a heel-long fur coat, a semi-round fur hat and a white *valenki* (high boots) with a silver or red ornament, a magical staff, and a *troika* (horse-drawn sleigh). While his robes are often red and gold, they were usually a light blue during the Soviet era, so as not to confuse him with the Western Santa Claus. If you want to find Ded Moroz's home, this is accepted to be in the wooded village of Veliky Ustyug, in the Vologodskaya region of northern Russia, about 500 miles northeast of Moscow – a little cold for some, but a bonus for the men of Russia, is that Ded Moroz is also assisted by a beautiful snow maiden called Snegurochka.

 Number of prisoners granted home leave for Christmas from Northern Ireland jails in 2005

QUOTE UNQUOTE

Now I'm an old Christmas tree, the roots of which have died. They just come along and while the little needles fall off me replace them with medallions.
Orson Welles, US actor, director and producer

ONE GIGANTIC PIE

'Huge meat pies were made that are unbelievable as to size and content,' says Alfred Carl Hottes in his festive compilation of *1001 Christmas Facts and Fancies*. In his account, he speaks of a gigantic pie baked for Sir Henry Grey on Twelfth Night, 1770, where 'the recipes of the chroniclers differ but all agree that it was nine feet in circumference and weighed 165 pounds' and 'served from a four-wheel cart built for the purpose'. According to Hottes, it contained approximately:

2 bushels of flour
20 pounds of butter
4 geese
2 rabbits
2 woodcocks
6 snipes
4 partridges
2 meat's tongues
6 pigeons
7 blackbirds

NATIVITY TRADITIONS OF THE WORLD: COLOMBIA

The Nativity scene is beloved by Christians around the world, with many cultures and customs 'making it their own'...

The Christmas decorations of Colombia, including the Nativity, are put in place on 8 December, a day known as *Dia de las Velitas* or Candle's Day. Traditionally, the scene is completed as time goes by, with Baby Jesus placed there on 24 December. The shepherds are then added on the following days and the wise men on 6 January or Epiphany. This scene is traditionally not taken down until 2 February or Candlemas – the end of Epiphany season.

Italian prisoner of war camp number in California that inspired the 1948 film Natale A Campo 119 *or* Christmas at Camp 119

A SONG FOR CHRISTMAS

Number one Christmas singles with a Christmas theme (as given by the official UK Singles Chart):

1955	Dickie Valentine	*Christmas Alphabet*
1957	Harry Belafonte	*Mary's Boy Child*
1973	Slade	*Merry Xmas Everybody*
1974	Mud	*Lonely this Christmas*
1976	Johnny Mathis	*When a Child is Born (Soleado)*
1978	Boney M	*Mary's Boy Child-Oh My Lord*
1984	Band Aid	*Do they Know it's Christmas*
1985	Shakin' Stevens	*Merry Christmas Everyone*
1988	Cliff Richard	*Mistletoe and Wine*
1989	Band Aid II	*Do they Know it's Christmas*
2004	Band Aid 20	*Do they Know it's Christmas*

CHRISTMAS CRACKERS

The ones you wish you'd never pulled...

JOKE: How many reindeer does it take to change a light bulb?

Answer on page 153

NO ROOM AT THE INN?

For those people who are homeless or living in hostel accommodation, Christmas can be a lonely or depressing time. But there are some people who are helping to provide room at the inn. For the past 36 years, Crisis Open Christmas, run by the homelessness charity Crisis, has helped to alleviate that loneliness in the UK capital, providing centres across London from 23-30 December each year. These centres offer companionship, hot meals and warmth plus a wide range of services that homeless people do not normally have access to. In 2007, over 7,500 volunteers gave up their time over the Christmas week to support their work. Their roles included welcoming guests and serving food, washing hair and sorting bedding, coordinating food deliveries, being a translator, assisting with medical care, providing entertainment and education and making sure centres are ready for guests. The application date for volunteers in 2008 was 1 October 2008 and a similar format runs each year. You can find out more at www.crisis.org.uk/page.builder/crisis_open_christmasnew.html.

 Number of years that a Christmas tree had remained in the Parker family in 2006, bought for six old pence in 1886

TALES OF CHRISTMAS PAST

Love came down at Christmas,
Love all lovely, love divine;
Love was born at Christmas;
Star and angels gave the sign.

Christina Rossetti, 'Love came down at Christmas', 1885

QUOTE UNQUOTE

In my experience, clever food is not appreciated at Christmas. It makes the little ones cry and the old ones nervous.
Jane Grigson, British food writer

IT'S CHRISTMAS UP IN SPACE

On Christmas Eve 1968, Commander Frank Borman, Command Pilot Jim Lovell and Lunar Module Pilot William Anders of the spaceship *Apollo 8* became the first astronauts to spend Christmas in space, and delivered the very first Christmas Eve broadcast from lunar orbit. The occasion had an estimated one billion people from around the world turn their TVs or radios to heaven and tune into Christmas greetings and live images from the astronauts to their home planet. The spacemen also read from the Book of Genesis, with Borman closing with the words: 'Good night, good luck, a Merry Christmas, and God bless all of you – all of you on the good Earth.' The ship then ended its history-making journey by splashing down in the Pacific Ocean on 27 December. It was 1973 before another crew spent Christmas in space, this time aboard the *Skylab 4*. Their Christmas celebration was more of a Warholesque event with Commander Gerald Carr, Pilot William Pogue and Scientist Edward Gibson making a Christmas tree from food cans. The third American Christmas outside the Earth's atmosphere took place when astronaut John Blaha celebrated the holiday in orbit on board the Russian *Mir* space station in 1996 – some 22 years later. More Christmas space missions would follow, with one of the best presents to the world given by crew on the *STS-103 Discovery* space shuttle. After three consecutive days of spacewalks to make repairs and upgrades, they returned the Hubble Space Telescope to service on Christmas Day 1999 – a gift to scientists and space fans worldwide.

DRESS YOUR DOOR

What's the best greenery for large wreaths? Any of the following, says Alfred Carl Hottes, author of the 1937 compendium *1001 Christmas Facts and Fancies*. Just take your pick...

White pine
Fir
Douglas-fir
Blue spruce
Boxwood
Oregon hollygrape
English ivy
Glossy privet
Galax
Southern evergreen Huckleberry
Groundpine
Mountain-laurel
American holly
English holly
Colorado juniper
Box
Arborvitae
Yew

THE NATIVITY: THE STAR OF BETHLEHEM

Some things you may or may not know about principal characters in the Nativity:

- According to the Gospel of St Matthew, the Magi were inspired by a star to travel to Jerusalem in search of the King of the Jews
- The Magi met King Herod in Jerusalem and told him about the rising of the star and their search
- Herod was frightened and from information given to him from his advisers, told the Magi that the child was in Bethlehem, hoping to trick them into showing him Jesus' whereabouts so that he could kill him
- St Matthew's account suggests that the Magi knew from the star that the King of the Jews had already been born, rather than leading them to his birth
- The star is a much disputed part of the Nativity: some refuse to believe that a star could pinpoint a place as exact as a house; others argue that the star was linked to astrology although the rest of the Bible condemns its use; further theories point to the star as an astronomical event such as a nova or comet or even that the star was an actual human guide who could lead the Magi to their destination; while most nativity plays use artistic license to include the star as a miraculous happening and often a human-sized one at that
- The Star of Bethlehem is also called the Christmas Star or Jesus Star
- Matthew is the only one of the four Gospels that mention either the Star of Bethlehem or the Magi

 Number of toy plane models – all the world's fighter planes – hung on the 2007 Tate Britain Christmas tree, by artist Fiona Banner

CHRISTMAS DINNER IN... FRANCE AND QUEBEC

On Christmas Day in France and Quebec you could be tucking into:

A *réveillon* (long dinner) of:

- Lobsters
- Oysters
- Escargots
- Foie gras
- Turkey stuffed with chestnuts
- *Tourtière* (meat pie made of ground pork, veal or beef – common in Quebec)
- *Bûche de Nöel* (Yule log)
- Champagne

QUOTE UNQUOTE

There's nothing sadder in this world than to awake Christmas morning and not be a child.
Erma Bombeck, US author and humorist

HOW TO... PLAY HOT COCKLES

A cross between 'blind man's bluff' and 'whodunnit', Hot Cockles was a popular Christmas party pastime during the 18th and 19th centuries. To play, simply nominate a person, blindfold them and make them kneel or lie face down in the centre of the room. Then get the other guests to take turns tapping the person on the shoulder until he guesses their name. When someone guesses correctly they take the place of the blindfolded and the game continues. This can then be made more interesting with forfeits for wrong guesses or mid-game misdemeanours. There can also be added interest if there is any fission in the room between participating members, as happened to one reader of *The Spectator* who recorded his experience of Hot Cockles in a letter to the magazine, in December 1711:

Mr Spectator,
I am a Footman in a great Family and am in Love with the House-maid. We were all at Hot-cockles last Night in the Hall thee Holidays; when I lay down and was blinded, she pull'd off her shoe, and hit me with the Heel such a Rap, as almost broke my Head to Pieces. Pray, Sir, was this Love or Spite?
T.

Number in millions of Christmas cards sent in London, in 2007, 123
according to Recycle for London

HERE WE COME A-WASSAILING

The word 'wassail' has come to be synonymous with Christmas as one way of 'wassailing' is to go from door to door singing Christmas carols. Wassailing is also commonly performed on Twelfth Night or around Epiphany, another key date in the Christmas calendar.

The word is said to stem from the Anglo Saxon toast *waes u hael*, translated as 'be thou hale' or 'be in good health'. Some word scholars go even further back and denote the Old Norse *ves heill* as the source of the Middle English *waeshaeil*. Either way, you end up with the same meaning – that of wishing good will.

In terms of wassailing and the various practices to which it is connected, good will is both given and sought. In the Middle Ages, peasants would seek food, drink and other gifts from their lords, in exchange for their blessings and good will. This began as a way to distinguish charitable giving from begging.

This is illustrated in that most famous wassailing song 'Here We Come A-Wassailing', when the wassailers would inform the lord of the house that 'we are not daily beggars that beg from door to door but we are friendly neighbours whom you have never seen before'. The song then goes on to show how the wassailers give 'Love and joy' to their lord, along with a 'God bless you' and 'send you a Happy New Year'; it is seen by some as a precursor to that popular Christmas carol and Hallmark phrase, 'We wish you a merry Christmas'.

Wassailing was not always a cordial affair, however, as the combination of alcohol and charitable extraction in wassailing times past did lead to rowdy bands of men entering the homes of wealthy neighbours and demanding free food and drink – anyone who said 'no' could have their house cursed or even vandalised. This is also represented in 'We wish you a merry Christmas' where singers won't leave until they get some figgy pudding.

Apple orchard wassailing in cider-producing areas of England was and is still done to toast the health of trees so that they might better thrive – and bring a great cider harvest in the autumn.

Singing and dancing along with drum banging and pot clanging is also said to scare away evil spirits. Proceedings are led by a wassail king and queen who are elected at the beginning of the ceremony. The wassail queen can be lifted up into the boughs of a tree, where she will place toast that has been soaked in wassail (spicy cider) in the branches, in order to show the spirits what a great harvest they have had.

It is said that this toast, also placed in the wassail cup to soak the intoxicating, spicy cider up, is also the origin of the 'toast' made to a fellow drinker just before you sup from your cups. Toasting, in this way, still lives on whether you have a cup of wassail or not.

 Number of the Antonov An-124 Ruslan plane that transported a 73ft Norwegian Christmas tree from Cleveland to New York in 1998

CHRISTMAS IN PICTURES

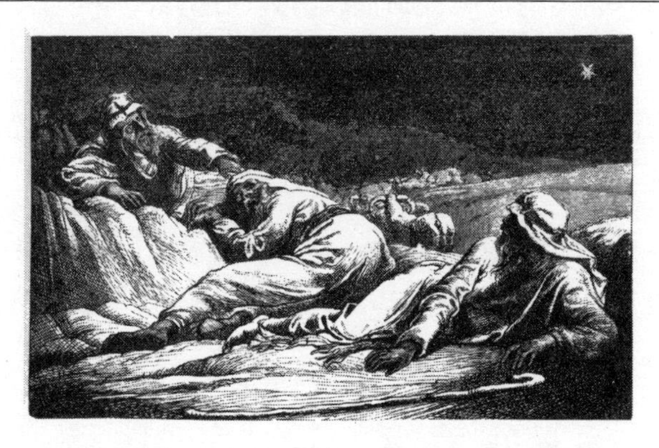

'I'm not following any ruddy star at 3am,' growled Bert. 'There's a perfectly good bus in the morning.'

GIVE A GOAT

Looking for a gift that makes a difference? Try World Vision's Alternative Gifts service at www.greatgifts.org. All gifts have been requested by one of the communities where World Vision is working so you can be assured that all gifts are wanted not wasted. Some Christmas highlights in 2007 included:

Gift	Price	Great for producing...
20 chickens	£14	Eggs and meat for the community in Chettikulam in Sri Lanka
A goat	£17	Milk and offspring to trade with other people in Hurungwe, Zimbabwe
School dinners	£28	School dinners for three children for a year, so they can go to school
60 fruit trees	£54	Healthy fruit for families to eat and sell in Mbella, Senegal
Pair of llamas	£90	Higher-quality wool for families to sell in the Cochabamba region of Bolivia
Train a teacher	£300	Well-trained teachers and improved lessons for the Daringbadi region of India

TALES OF CHRISTMAS PAST

Chapter 11: 'How the First Stockings Were Hung by the Chimneys'

Now it was on this same Christmas Eve that little Margot and her brother Dick and her cousins Ned and Sara, who were visiting at Margot's house, came in from making a snow man, with their clothes damp, their mittens dripping and their shoes and stockings wet through and through. They were not scolded, for Margot's mother knew the snow was melting, but they were sent early to bed that their clothes might be hung over chairs to dry. The shoes were placed on the red tiles of the hearth, where the heat from the hot embers would strike them, and the stockings were carefully hung in a row by the chimney, directly over the fireplace. That was the reason Santa Claus noticed them when he came down the chimney that night and all the household were fast asleep. He was in a tremendous hurry and seeing the stockings all belonged to children he quickly stuffed his toys into them and dashed up the chimney again, appearing on the roof so suddenly that the reindeer were astonished at his agility.

"I wish they would all hang up their stockings," he thought, as he drove to the next chimney. "It would save me a lot of time and I could then visit more children before daybreak."

L Frank Baum, *The Life and Adventures of Santa Claus*, 1902

BEST OF BRANDY

It's a cold winter's day. You want to warm the cockles of your heart. You head for the drinks cabinet to find a suitable drink. Gin, no, white wine, no, vodka, no... ahhh, brandy! A shot of smooth, full-flavoured brandy can quickly put the Christmas spirit back into you, but it's not all about the inebriation. Scientists recently found that brandy could actually benefit your health too. In 2005, researchers at Monash University School of Physics found that good-quality brandy contained health-giving antioxidants obtained mainly from the copper during the distilling process. Team leader Dr Troup said that 30ml of brandy would give the equivalent antioxidant potential as the daily recommended intake of vitamin C. And while these antioxidants make up only a small percentages of substances found in brandy, they are a very important part of the mix. Brandy should be drunk 'in moderation' of course, reiterated Dr Troup. As should dollops of Christmas brandy butter, brandy sauce and brandy cake if you want to keep a wandering waistline down.

 Width in millimetres of The Best of Mrs Beeton's Christmas, *published in November 2007 and containing over 200 recipes*

GIFTS FOR A BABY?

Biblical descriptions of the nativity tell us that the Magi – or 'Three Kings' – brought three gifts to the baby Jesus. While it can be agreed that none of the gifts were particularly useful for a baby, the symbolism of these gifts varies from tradition to tradition. Some thoughts are:

Gift	**Given by**	**Symbolism/use of gift**
Gold	Melchior	Valuable, Kingship on earth, Virtue
Frankincense	Balthasar	Perfume/incense, Priestship, Prayer
Myrhh	Caspar	Annointing/embalming oil, Death, Suffering

WHEN ONE TREE IS NOT ENOUGH

Not content with one Christmas tree, David Blair's collection numbered 26 in December 2007, and all inside his two-bedroom Studio City home, Los Angeles. As reported by the *LA Times*, Blair cheerfully admitted that: 'There are trees in every room, even the kitchen and bath. It's kind of an obsession.' Entry to his home would render this an understatement. His collection includes 10,000 ornaments, used to decorate an antique tree with a spun glass butterfly from the 1920s, a brown glass bunny and black glass tea and coffee pots from his grandparents' ornament collection; an Asian-themed tree hung with fragile pagodas, lanterns, kimonos and ginger jars; the main tree with silver, blue and white ornaments, all apparently very meaningful; a pair of dining room trees with Italian glass fruit and vegetables; twig trees in the bathroom; a very male tree in the master bedroom – black and loaded with yellow and white taxicabs – in tribute to Blair's partner, Dan Darwish, who collects ceramic cars; and a kid-friendly kitsch tree with brown fabric monkeys and yellow glass bananas. Friends have dubbed Blair the Hollywood Christmas Guy, and he has now turned his hobby into a home-based business of the same name, decorating trees for parties. Blair's obsession began at the age of five, when his mother (a collector of decorative eggs) and his grandmother (an ornament collector) gave him a four-foot brush tree to decorate. He's certainly added some tinsel since his first tentative decorations made out of popcorn garlands, and now entertains more than 300 guests each year who come to gaze in awe at his trees.

Amount in pounds sterling spent on girls at Christmas, compared to 127 *£223 on boys, according to a 2005 Woolworths poll*

A FORFEIT SIR!

Parlour games were popular during Victorian times, especially at Christmas. And along with parlour games, came forfeits for those questions got wrong or losers of the games. According to Cassell's Household Guide to Every Department of Practical Life *(1900) a few Victorian forfeits for gentlemen include:*

- To kiss every lady 'in the Spanish Fashion'. This is where one of the ladies accompanies him round the room and does all the kissing on his behalf, then wipes his mouth with a handkerchief
- To make a Grecian statue. The victim stands on a chair and has his limbs put into whatever pose the company chooses
- To say half a dozen flattering things to a lady without using the letter L
- To go round the room blindfolded and kiss all the ladies. The trick being that when the blindfold goes on, all the ladies switch places with each other and with the gentlemen

FESTIVE FLORA AND FAUNA: THE DONKEY

Perhaps the most popular representation of the Christmas donkey is in the song 'Little Donkey'. 'Plodding onwards' with his 'precious load', this little donkey is there to get Mary to Bethlehem in order that she can give birth to Jesus – or so the Bible story goes. Another Bible story tells of Jesus riding a donkey into Jerusalem, a few days before his crucifixion. In fact, the word 'donkey' is a relatively new one, first appearing as recently as the 18th century. In the Hebrew Bible, the 'donkey' is actually referred to as *hamor* or *charmor*; in later translated versions, it is called a 'colt'. While modern depictions are of the donkey as a lowly animal, at the time of Christ's birth it used to be an animal of some prestige, indicating a rider's high standing in the world. When the donkey became more of a 'beast of burden' figure, some Bible readers came to view riding on a donkey as a sign of a person's humility. Still others believe that the 'colt' mentioned in the Bible could well have been a horse, although this animal was often associated with war while the donkey represents peace. Legend also has it that the cross-like markings on the donkey's shoulders come from the shadow of Christ's crucifixion, placing the donkey at the foot of the cross; or that it is the mark left by a heavily pregnant Mary, while out 'on the dusty road'.

 Number of Bach Cantata played on the BBC Radio 3's A Bach Christmas *show, during the Christmas season of 2005*

QUOTE UNQUOTE

I have only one firm belief about the American political system, and that is this: God is a Republican and Santa Claus is a Democrat.
PJ O'Rourke, US political satirist

CHRISTMAS CRACKERS

The ones you wish you'd never pulled...

JOKE: Which of Santa's reindeer has bad manners?

Answer on page 153

BEST-SELLING ALBUMS OF CHRISTMAS PAST – 1990S

From the British Library's *Pop Goes the Library* exhibition in association with The Official UK Charts Company, 26 July 2006 to 25 March 2007. More than 20% of albums are sold in December alone, many ending up in Christmas stockings.

1990	*The Immaculate Collection*	Madonna
1991	*Greatest Hits II*	Queen
1992	*Cher's Greatest Hits: 1965-1992*	Cher
1993	*Bat Out of Hell II – Back Into Hell*	Meat Loaf
1994	*Carry On Up the Charts – The Best of the Beautiful South*	The Beautiful South
1995	*Robson & Jerome*	Robson & Jerome
1996	*Spice*	Spice Girls
1997	*Lets Talk About Love*	Celine Dion
1998	*Ladies & Gentlemen – The Best of George Michael*	George Michael
1999	*Come on Over*	Shania Twain

Episode number of 'Christmas Flintstone' from the animated TV series
The Flintstones, *where Fred works as a department store Santa*

CHRISTMAS DINNER IN... DENMARK

On Christmas Day in Denmark you could be tucking into:

- Roast pork, goose or duck
- Potatoes
- Red cabbage
- Gravy
- Rice pudding (often with an almond inside)
- *Glögg* (mulled wine with almonds and raisins)
- Christmas beer (specially brewed for a higher alcohol content)

SANTA LUCIA

Sweden prides itself on being one of the world's most egalitarian countries, but once a year all this goes to pot with the competition to find the national and the local Santa Lucia for the annual festival on Christmas Eve. According to Agneta Lilja, a lecturer in ethnology at Södertön University College, the festival of Santa Lucia stems back to the story of St Lucia of Syracuse, a martyr who died in the year AD304. Swedish legend also has Lucia as Adam's first wife, a woman who consorted with the devil and spawned a host of invisible infernals. The name is therefore associated with both light (lux) and Satan (Lucifer) with present customs appearing to blend both traditions. Lucia Night used to be the longest night of the year, when supernatural beings entered the world and all animals could speak. By morning, livestock needed extra feed and people needed extra nourishment, and were urged to eat several hearty breakfasts. This kind of feasting presaged the Christmas fast that happened on Lucia Day. The last person to rise on Lucia morning was nicknamed 'Lusse the Louse' and often playfully beat around the legs with birch twigs. Young people would then dress up as Lucia figures (*lussegubbar*) and wander from house to house singing songs and scrounging for food and schnapps. This custom virtually disappeared with urban migration, and white-clad Lucias took their place, singing songs and wearing the now customary crown of candles or lights. The first recorded appearance of such a figure was in a country house in 1764, and Stockholm proclaimed its first Lucia in 1927. Since 1888, Lucia has also been serving up saffron buns shaped like curled-up cats with raisin eyes (*lussekatter*) and coffee or *glögg*. Alongside midsummer, the Santa Lucia is now Sweden's foremost celebration, taking precedence over Christmas Day.

 Number of Christmas cards sent by the Doherty family each year according to a 2006 interview with Pete Doherty's mum, Jacqueline

WITH THIS TREE, WE THEE HONOUR

Some civic Christmas trees are presented as gifts by other towns or countries. Here are some of the reasons why...

Location: Trafalgar Square, London
Presented by: City of Oslo, Norway
With thanks for: British support of Norwegian resistance during World War II

Location: Boston
Presented by: Province of Nova Scotia
With thanks for: Rapid deployment of supplies and rescuers to the 1917 ammunition ship explosion that levelled the city of Halifax

Location: Newcastle-upon-Tyne
Presented by: Bergen, Norway
With thanks for: The part played by soldiers from Newcastle in liberating Bergen from Nazi occupation

HOW TO... FORCE A TURKEY

Some people always know best, especially when it comes to Christmas Day cooking, and such was the case for one Mrs Glasse, writing in The Art of Cookery Made Plain and Easy *in 1755.*

The best way to roast a turkey is to loosen the skin on the Breast of the Turkey, and fill it with ForceMeat, made thus: Take a Quarter of a Pound of Beef Sewet, as many Crumbs of Bread, a little Lemon peel, an Anchovy, some Nutmeg, Pepper, Parsley and a little Thyme. Chop and beat them all well together, mix them with the Yolk of an Egg, and stuff up the Breast; when you have no Sewet, Butter will do; or you may make your Force Meat thus: Spread Bread and Butter thin, and grate some Nutmeg over it; when you have enough to roll it up, and stuff the Breast of the Turkey; then roast it of a fine Brown, but be sure to pin some white Paper on the Breast till it is near enough. You must have a good gravy in the Dish, and Bread-Sauce, made thus: Take a good piece of Crumb put it into a pint of Water, with a blade or two of Mace, two or three Cloves, and some Whole Pepper. Boil it up five or six times, then with a spoon take out the Spice you had before put in, and then you must pour off the Water (you may boil an Onion in it if you please) then beat up the Bread with a good Piece of Butter and a little Salt.

THE TEN PEAKS OF CHRISTMAS

The Christmas Mountains are a series of rounded peaks at the headwaters of North Pole Stream and the Little Southwest Miramichi River in New Brunswick, Canada. A sub-range of the Appalachians, they were named in 1964 by one Arthur F Wightman, who linked the words North Pole Stream with Christmas through their shared connection with reindeers. The 10 mountains in the range include:

Mount	Height
Mount Cupid	530m
Mount Comet	550m
Mount Prancer	580m
Mount St Nicholas	625m
Mount Vixen	650m
Mount Blitzen	670m
Mount Dancer	670m
North Pole Mountain	690m
Mount Donder	730m
Mount Dasher	750m

A ROYAL RESTING PLACE

Many people believe that they have seen the final resting place of the Magi, described in the Bible as visiting Jesus after his birth. These include:

Marco Polo

He claimed that he was shown the three tombs of the Magi at Saveh, south of Tehran in the 1270s. In his book *The Book of the Million*, book i., he states: 'In Persia is the city of Saba, from which the Three Magi set out and in this city they are buried, in three very large and beautiful monuments, side by side. And above them there is a square building, beautifully kept. The bodies are still entire, with hair and beard remaining.'

St Helena

She claims that she found the bones of the 'Three Wise Men' while on her famous pilgrimage to Palestine and the Holy Lands. She then took the remains to the church of Hagia Sophia in Constantinople. They were later moved to Milan and currently reside in the Shrine of the Three Kings at Cologne Cathedral, having been sent there by the Holy Roman Emperor Frederick I in AD1164.

 Percentage rise in UK sales of champagne over the Christmas period in 2000, according to a drinks marketing survey

QUOTE UNQUOTE

For mixing the pudding you need a really capacious bowl and a stout wooden spoon – and as everybody in the family is supposed to take a hand in the job, this part of it shouldn't be very hard work.

Elizabeth David, British cookery writer, talking about the stirring of the Christmas pudding

TALES OF CHRISTMAS PAST

Her visitor was a tall, thin man, and he had a slouch hat, which he held in his hands as he talked. He seemed nervous, and his face wore a worried look—extremely worried. He looked like a man who had lost nine hundred dollars, but he did not look like Santa Claus. He was thinner and not so jolly-looking. At first Mrs. Gratz had no idea that Santa Claus was standing before her, for he did not have a sleigh-bell about him, and he had left his red cotton coat with the white batting trimming at home. He stood in the door playing with his hat, unable to speak. He seemed to have some delicacy about beginning.

"Well, what it is?" said Mrs. Gratz.

Her visitor pulled himself together with an effort.

"Well, ma'am, I'll tell you," he said frankly. "I'm a chicken buyer. I buy chickens. That's my business—dealin' in poultry—so I came out to-day to buy some chickens—"

"On Christmas Day?" asked Mrs. Gratz.

"Well," said the man, moving uneasily from one foot to the other, "I did come on Christmas Day, didn't I? I don't deny that, ma'am. I did come on Christmas Day. I'd like to go out and have a look at your chickens—"

"It ain't so usual for buyers to come buying chickens on Christmas Day, is it?" interposed Mrs. Gratz, good-naturedly.

"Well, no, it ain't, and that's a fact," said the man uneasily. "But I always do. The people I buy chickens for is just as apt to want to eat chicken one day as another day—and more so. Turkey on Christmas Day, and chicken the next, for a change—that's what they always tell me. So I have to buy chickens every day. I hate to, but I have to, and if I could just go out and look around your chicken yard—"

It was right there that Mrs. Gratz had a suspicion that Santa Claus stood before her.

Ellis Parker Butler, 'The Thin Santa Claus', first published in the *Saturday Evening Post*, 1908

Number in millions of US consumers out Christmas shopping on Black Friday – the busiest shopping day of the year – in 2007 133

A potted history of the Christmas pantomime

Grecian roots

A *pantominos* in Greece originally described a solo dancer who 'imitated all'; this stems from the words *panto* for 'all' and *mimos* for 'mimic'. The pantominos' often effeminate dance would be accompanied by sung narrative and instrumental music. The word took on a life of its own and was soon applied to the performance itself, with the fusion of comedy and tragedy becoming an extremely popular form of entertainment in ancient Greece and Rome.

Clowning around

Modern pantomine also has strong links with the *Commedia dell' Arte*. This form of popular theatre began in Italy in the early Middle Ages and reached England by the 16th century. The name translates as a 'comedy of professional artists', who would travel from province to province in Italy and France, telling stories along the way but improvising and changing the main character to suit the location and crowd. The great clown Grimaldi then transformed the format to include standard characters such as lovers, a father and servants, often one sly and one foolish. It is this format that forms the basis of pantomime today.

Gender bending

Some say the idea of role reversal in pantomime – where an actress plays the principal man and an actor plays the dame – stems from the old festival of Twelfth Night. This was a combination of Epiphany and the midwinter solstice when it was customary for the natural order of things to be reversed. However, it was often common for a man to play a woman in Shakespearean times when it was not socially accepted for women to appear on the stage. The clown Grimaldi is attributed with being the first official 'pantomime dame' with his stage performances as Queen Rondabellyana in *Harlequin and the Red Dwarf* and Dame Cecily Suet in *Harlequin Whittington* in the 1800s.

Operatic illusions

Pantomime in Britain began life as bite-sized performances between opera pieces, but eventually found a footing for its own show. It was considered a low form of opera, rather like the *Commedia dell' Arte* but without the Harlequin. That is, until actor, manager and widely accepted 'Father of Pantomime' John Rich brought in his Harlequin equivalent, under the name of Lun (short for lunatic) in 1716. This didn't elevate pantomime to the elite rafters occupied by opera. But it did produce a wildly popular form of entertainment that, through key performances at Lincoln's Inn, Drury Lane, Sadlers Wells, and then popularised through Victorian Music Hall, took on the comedic format it is today.

 Number of recipes in the DVD Delia Smith – The Ultimate Delia, *including her entire Christmas collection, covering 36 hours before the day*

HAPPY E-MAS

Christmas e-card images from the British Library, 2007

- Capricorn
- Nativity 1
- Nativity 2
- Flight into Egypt
- Igloos
- Adoration of the Magi 1
- Adoration of the Magi 2
- Virgin Mary and Child
- Annunciation to the Shepherds
- Mr Fezziwig's Ball
- Buckingham House
- Night Before Christmas
- Chopping Logs
- Robin
- Christmas Merry-Making

A FORFEIT, MADAM!

Parlour games were especially popular during Victorian times, especially at Christmas. And along with parlour games, came forfeits for those questions got wrong or losers of the games. According to Cassell's *Household Guide to Every Department of Practical Life* (1900), a few Victorian forfeits for ladies include:

- To stand in the middle of the room and spell 'opportunity'. Then, if one of the gentlemen can catch her before she manages to sit down 'he may avail himself of the opportunity offered, under the mistletoe'
- To answer 'yes' or 'no' to three questions. The lady leaves the room while everyone agrees on what questions to ask. 'Ladies of experience say the right answer is no'
- To kiss a gentleman 'rabbit fashion'. The lady is allowed her choice of gentleman, then they each put one end of a piece of cotton in their respective mouths and nibble towards each other until they're kissing
- To kiss the gentleman you love best in the company, without anyone knowing it. The idea being that the only way to do this is to kiss all of them
- To kiss each corner of the room. Which sounds innocuous enough – except that four gentlemen immediately station themselves in the corners, lips puckered and whiskers a-quiver

CHRISTMAS CRACKERS

The ones you wish you'd never pulled...

JOKE: How do cats greet each other at Christmas?

Answer on page 153

RUDOLPH THE RED-NOSED REINDEER ROCKS

Just some of the bands and singers who couldn't resist doing a cover of the red-nosed song:

Johnny Marks (first appearance as a song in 1949)
Gene Autry
Smashing Pumpkins
Destiny's Child
Burl Ives

CHRISTMAS COMES EARLY FOR LYME REGIS

Lyme Regis is a popular UK holiday spot, thanks to the spectacular scenery and fossil findings along the Jurassic Coast, and for the unique stone harbour cobb made famous by John Fowles' book *The French Lieutenant's Woman*. But on Christmas Eve 1839, an occurrence happened that really put Lyme Regis on the map – the Bindon Landslide. Described by two eminent scientists of their day, William Conybeare and William Buckland, the landslide was of a type known as a blockside. A huge piece of land, known locally as Goat Island, moved towards the sea, leaving a deep chasm. Over eight million tons of land was dislodged, creating an enormous chasm with cliff-like walls over 150ft high. Mysteriously, the corn that had previously grown on much of the land continued to grow in the gulf left by the landslide, while the front edge of the landslide was uplifted out of the sea and formed a small natural harbour. Although the latter proved a short-lived feature, Parliament did question whether it could become a port for the Navy. It didn't but the site did attract national publicity and thousands of visitors, with people coming in droves by paddle steamer. A piece of music was even written for it called the 'Landslide Quadrille', along with many beautiful prints and engravings, and framed ears of corn sold as souvenirs. In one way, it was Christmas come early for the shopkeepers of this part of the coast.

 Number of Christmas trees stolen by a youth from Queens, New York, in 1982, taken from the Friendly Frost Garden Center

DREAMING OF A WHITE CHRISTMAS

White Christmases are a relatively rare occurrence these days but still, when many of us think of Christmas, we think of snow. The origins of the white Christmas stem from a time when Britain had a colder climate, a time some refer to as the 'Little Ice Age', between 1550 and 1850. According to the Met Office, winters were particularly severe then, with some winters, such as the one in 1814, being so cold that a frost fair could be held on the frozen River Thames – an elephant was even led over the river under Blackfriars Bridge. Today, snow is more likely to come in the deepening cold of January. Christmas comes at the beginning of the season, so often misses out. Our Christmas Day is also 12 days prior to the one in 1752, when the change of calendar brought everything back, giving us even less chance of a white Christmas. However, there is some hope in the most widely used definition of a white Christmas by those placing and taking bets. Instead of a white Christmas meaning a complete covering of snow that ideally falls between midnight and midday of the 25 December, a 'white Christmas' is defined as a single snowflake observed falling in the 24 hours of 25 December. The last time this happened was in 2004, when snow was widespread across Northern Ireland, Scotland, parts of Wales, the Midlands, northeast, and far southwest of England.

TALES OF CHRISTMAS PAST

Last letter

I am so glad you did not forget to write me again this year. The number of children who keep up with me seems to be getting smaller. I expect it is because of this horrible war, and that when it is over things will improve again, and I shall be busy as ever. But at present so terribly many people have lost their homes, or left them; half the world seems in the wrong place! And even up here we have been having troubles. I don't mean only with my stores; of course they are getting low. They were already last year, and I have not been able to fill them up, so that I have now to send what I can, instead of what is asked for. But worse than that had happened.

...I suppose after this year you will not be hanging your stocking any more. I shall have to say 'goodbye', more or less: I mean, I shall not forget you. We always keep the names of our old friends, and their letters; and later on we hope to come back when they are grown up and have houses of their own and children...

JRR Tolkien, *The Father Christmas Letters*, 1976

Run time in minutes of the DVD Jamie's Christmas, *with tips and advice* 137 *including Jamie Oliver's favourite turkey with all the trimmings*

WHILE SHEPHERDS WATCHED THEIR FLOCKS BY NIGHT

Artists who have famously depicted the Biblical Adoration of the Shepherds in paintings and sculpture, in churches, and in other buildings:

- (Antonio Allergri da) Correggio
- (Michelangelo Merisi da) Caravaggio
- Domenico Ghirlandaio
- Giorgione (or Giorgio Barbarelli da Castelfranco)
- Giotto (di Bondone)
- Hugo van der Goes
- El Greco (or Doménicos Theotokópoulos)
- Georges de la Tour
- Andrea Mantegna
- Bartolomé Esteban Murillo
- Nichlas Poussin
- Rembrandt (Harmenszoon van Rijn)
- Martin Schongauer
- Edward Burne-Jones

FOR THE LOVE OF LIGHTS

Heard the one about the man with 10,000 lights on his house? He paid £700 for Southern Electricity to install a factory-strength 145-amp power line to ensure fans of his annual display – dubbed the 'Melksham Illuminations' – wouldn't be disappointed. *Metro* reported in December 2007 that Alex Goodhind, a 23-year-old electrician, was using so much power that he was unable to boil a kettle when the lights were in full effect. He also spent five weeks putting up the decorations and added £500 to his electricity bill over the three-week festive period during which they were switched on. Plus an extra £2,000 went on additional lights this year to the delight of his daily crowd of 300 visitors. While some might say the lights are a waste of valuable fuel, electricity and money, not to mention a bit of an eyesore to those not comfortable with such blatant kitsch, Mr Goodhind defended his actions by saying: 'A lot of local organisations make minibus trips to see the lights. But we don't mind the popularity because it gives so much joy to so many people.' According to his father Colin, 57, Alex started putting up the lights when he was about 10. Bar a few embarrassing moments, the family have grown to love the display which, in 2007, raised £3,000 for a local hospice.

 Number of days left to Christmas, as exposed by The Guardian *in 2006, as Harrods launched its 'blizzard of baubles' on 8 August 2006*

THE NATIVITY: THE MAGI

Some things you may or may not know about principal characters in the Nativity:

- In the Bible the Gospel of St Matthew states that the Magi came from the east to Jerusalem to worship the Christ, born King of the Jews
- Matthew also states that they navigated their way to Jesus by following a star which came to be known as the Star of Bethlehem
- The Magi's visit to Jesus is the first mention of his being in Bethlehem
- However the Gospel of St Matthew says that the Magi visited Jesus, not in a stable, but in a house. Some Christians dispute where or whose this house is
- As the Magi approached Jerusalem, Herod tried to trick them into revealing where Jesus was, so that he may put him to death
- The Bible tells us that after visiting Jesus, the Magi are warned in dreams of Herod's deadly intentions for him and decide to return home by a different route – Herod then decides to kill all the young children in Bethlehem to try and get rid of Jesus, no matter what the cost
- In Christian tradition the Magi are also known as the Wise Men, the Kings or the Kings from the east
- The number of Magi, Wise Men or Kings is commonly referred to as three. In fact the Bible never states how many Magi there were
- The number three may have come from the description of the symbolic gifts that the Magi brought: Gold, Frankincense and Myrrh – three in total
- The word 'Magi' is a Latinisation of the Greek word *magos*. This term is a specific occupational title referring to the priestly caste of Zoroastrianism
- Zoroastrian priests paid particular attention to the stars and gained an international reputation for astrology
- Matthew doesn't state exactly where the Magi come. He does say 'from the east' and from 'their own country'
- Some Christian traditions believe that the Magi were Persian, hence the clothes that they are usually depicted in
- The Western names of the Magi – Caspar, Melchior and Balthasar – have only been settled from the 8th century, from a Greek manuscript found in Alexandria

Approximate length in kilometres of the coastline of the Australian territory of Christmas Island

BIRTHS OF CHRISTMAS PAST

Historic and celebrity births that took place on Christmas Day...

1642	Sir Isaac Newton, English physicist and mathematician
1863	Charles Pathé, French pioneer of film and record industries
1876	Muhammad Ali Jinnah, founder of Pakistan
1887	Conrad Hilton, US hotelier
1899	Humphrey Bogart, US actor
1908	Quentin Crisp, British author
1911	Louise Bourgeois, sculptor
1944	Kenny Everett, British entertainer
1947	Nawaz Sharif, Prime Minister of Pakistan
1948	Sissy Spacek, US actress
1954	Annie Lennox, Scottish singer
1957	Shane MacGowan, Irish musician
1968	Helena Christensen, Danish model

SNACK ON... MRS BEETON'S MINCE PIES

Advice on how best to prepare mince pies, from Mrs Beeton's Book of Household Management *(1861) by Isabella Mary Mason Beeton (1836-1865):*

1311

Ingredients:- Good puff-paste No. 1205, mincemeat No. 1309.

Mode: Make some good puff-paste by recipe No. 1205; roll it out to the thickness of about ½ inch, and line some good-sized pattypans with it; fill them with mincemeat, cover with the paste, and cut it off all round close to the edge of the tin. Put the pies into a brisk oven, to draw the paste up, and bake for 25 minutes, or longer, should the pies be very large; brush them over with the white of an egg, beaten with the blade of a knife to a stiff froth; sprinkle over pounded sugar, and put them into the oven for a minute or two, to dry the egg; dish the pies on a white d'oyley, and serve hot. They may be merely sprinkled with pounded sugar instead of being glazed, when that mode is preferred. To re-warm them, put the pies on the pattypans, and let them remain in the oven for 10 minutes or ¼ hour, and they will be almost as good as if freshly made.

Time: 25 to 30 minutes; 10 minutes to re-warm them.

Average cost: 4d. each.

Sufficient: ½ lb. of paste for 4 pies.

Seasonable at Christmastime.

140 *Series number of Royal Mail presentation pack issued on 17 November 1982, displaying stamps with Christmas carol designs*

QUOTE UNQUOTE

My first copies of Treasure Island *and* Huckleberry Finn *still have some blue-spruce needles scattered in the pages. They smell of Christmas still.*
Charlton Heston, US actor

CHRISTMAS DINNER IN... CANADA

On Christmas Day in Canada you could be tucking into:

- Turkey
- Stuffing
- Mashed potatoes
- Gravy
- Cranberry sauce
- Vegetables
- Plum pudding
- Eggnog (milk-based punch)
- Butter tarts
- Shortbread

TO EAT HUMBLE PIE

'You need to eat some humble pie!' she cried, or so the idiom goes. Today we translate this as an instruction to obtain some humility, get off our high horses and stop being complacent or egotistical. But the humble pie to which it refers – a 17th-century Christmas food among lower-class peoples, as evidenced when Oliver Cromwell and the Puritans outlawed it along with other Christmas traditions – is actually an adaptation of umble pie, where the 'umble' evolved from 'numble' (after the French *nomble*) and meant 'deer's innards'. Umbles were considered inferior food and included liver, heart and other offal, especially of cow but often of deer or boar. Umble pie took all these umbles and encased them in a kind of pastry, to render a meat dish similar to a Cornish pasty. Although the medieval umble pies contained mostly tripe, they later evolved to include fruit and sweetening. Some even lost their umbles altogether bringing forth a relation of today's mince pie. So next time someone says 'Go eat some humble pie' you can go and do just that, and indulge a sweet tooth at the same time.

Age in years of a post office in the US town of Santa Claus, in a 1997
New York Times *article that told how staff coped with the Xmas post*

A TREE BY ANY OTHER NAME: NORTHERN EUROPE

Just when you thought picking up a Christmas tree was an easy game, choice came along to confuse matters. Apparently, it's a matter of which needle size, colour, shape and even scent of tree you prefer. Here are just some of the species of Christmas tree offered in Northern Europe...

Silver fir	*Abies alba*
Nordmann fir	*Abies nordmanniana*
Noble fir	*Abies procera*
Norway spruce	*Picea abies*
Serbian spruce	*Picea omorika*
Scots pine	*Pinus sylvestris*
Stone pine	*Pinus pinea*
Swiss pine	*Pinus cembra*

ROCKING THE CRADLE OF CHRISTIANITY

In December 2007, not all was well in Bethlehem's Church of the Nativity. As reported by *The Times* on 29 December, there was 'an unholy punch-up when Greek Orthodox and Armenian priests came to blows in a dispute over how to clean Bethlehem's Church of the Nativity'.

The brawl apparently began when Greek Orthodox priests set up ladders to clean the walls and ceilings of their part of the church after the Christmas Day celebrations. Armenian priests claimed that the ladders encroached on their portion of the church and this led to angry words between the two sects that quickly changed to blows.

Witnesses said that the robed and bearded priests scuffled for more than an hour, using fists, brooms and iron rods as weapons, with the fight eventually broken up by a dozen unarmed Palestinian police. The Mayor of Bethlehem, Victor Batarseh, seemed used to the problem saying: 'As usual the cleaning of the church after Christmas is a cause of problems'.

While tensions run high in the West Bank due to ongoing political problems, it is hoped that another ladder that led to a holy scuffle will serve as a reminder to keepers of the Church to solve their disputes in a more Christian manner. This ladder stands in the Church of the Holy Sepulchre in Jerusalem's Old City as a reminder of a fight caused by a priest attempting to repair damage done during an earthquake. Hopefully, somewhere along the line, the cycle of holy rage can be broken.

 Run time in minutes of a 2003 remake of A Christmas Carol, *starring* Star Trek *actor William Shatner*

LUCKY PUDS

Victorian tradition dictates that six objects be found in a Christmas pudding, each symbolising some good luck or charm for the future of their finders.

Two rings	To bring love
A sixpence	As a sign of prosperity
A trouser button	For the bachelor
A thimble	For the spinster or for thrift
A little pig	To determine the glutton at the table

CHRISTMAS CRACKERS

The ones you wish you'd never pulled...

JOKE: What do monkeys sing at Christmas?

Answer on page 153

HOW TO... MAKE A SNOWFLAKE

Ten steps to cheap but pretty Christmas decorations that recycle A4 paper too.

1) Take an A4 piece of paper and cut it to make a square
2) Fold it in half so that you have a triangle
3) Fold this in half to make a smaller triangle
4) Hold this triangle so that its longest side is at the top
5) Fold the right-hand corner into the middle so that it is directly above the bottom point of the triangle and press firmly
6) Fold the left-hand corner into the middle so that it crosses over the right-hand point and press firmly. You should be left with two points overlapping on the long side of the triangle
7) Cut off the two points that cross over the long side of the triangle. You should be left with another triangle. The tallest point will be the centre of your snowflake
8) Now cut out your pattern making sure that you leave at least some of the folded edges of the triangle intact so that your flake doesn't fall apart
9) Unfold your snowflake
10) Decorate them with glitter or paint, or leave them plain; string them together or stick them on windows so that the light shines through; enjoy them all Christmas through

CHRISTMAS ISLAND

There are several Christmas Islands in the world – and thankfully for the residents, these islands don't just come round but once a year:

Name of island: The Territory of Christmas Island
Nationality: Australian
Location: Indian Ocean, 2,600km northwest of Perth and 500km south of Jakarta

British and Dutch navigators first included this Christmas Island on their charts in the early 17th century. The island was named by Captain William Mynors of the British East India Company, who arrived there on Christmas Day 1643, on board the *Royal Mary*, However, the first recorded visit by William Dampier in March 1688 lists the island as uninhabited.

Due to the island's isolated position and rugged coast it was almost another 200 years before the first explorations discovered a workable anchorage – Flying Fish Cove, also known as Kampong – and began to record flora, fauna and minerals. On discovering some nearly pure phosphate of lime, the British Crown annexed the island on 6 June 1888. A small settlement was established soon after and mining began, using indentured labour from China, Malaysia and Singapore, in the 1890s.

In 1942, the island was invaded and occupied by the Japanese. Residents were interned until the end of World War II in 1945. Sovereignty was then transferred from the UK to Australia. Their first representative arrived in 1958 and now along with Cocos (Keeling) Island, Christmas Island forms part of the Australian Indian Ocean Territories.

Today the estimated population of Christmas Island is 1,493 with a mixed ethnicity of 70% Chinese, 20% European and 10% Malay. Together they occupy around 52 square miles of tropical rainforest terrain where 65% is now National Park. But perhaps the most famous inhabitant of the island is the Christmas Island red crab.

Ferns, orchids, vines and seabirds are in abundance but the red crab takes the biscuit with an annual mass migration that involves 100 million of its kind heading to the sea to spawn. This happens around November time, after the start of the wet season and in synch with the full moon.

The Red-footed Booby bird is also something of a celebrity on Christmas Island, with the territory providing the only nesting habitat in the world for its sister of the species, the Abbott's Booby, and for the endangered Christmas Island Frigatebird. Without these, Christmas Island just wouldn't be the same.

 Distance in miles north of the Equator, of Kiritimati, also known as Christmas Island, in the Indian Ocean

CHRISTMAS IN PICTURES

In the midst of the credit crunch, Lucia had to applaud her son's thriftiness in using roadkill for Christmas decorations.

QUOTE UNQUOTE

Were I a philosopher, I should write a philosophy of toys, showing that nothing else in life need to be taken seriously, and that Christmas Day in the company of children is one of the few occasions on which men become entirely alive.
Robert Lynd, US sociologist

TWELFTH NIGHT ROLE PLAY

Key characters from the Shakespeare play *Twelfth Night*:

Viola (aka Cesario)	Twin sister to Sebastian
Orsino	Duke or Count of Illyria
Lady Olivia	A Countess
Sebastian	Twin brother to Viola
Maria	A gentlewoman in Olivia's household
Sir Toby Belch	Olivia's relative (possibly uncle)
Sir Andrew Aguecheek	A knight and companion of Sir Toby's
Malvolio	Olivia's steward
Feste (the Fool)	A jester in Olivia's household
Fabian	Part of Olivia's household
Antonio	Sebastian's friend and rescuer
Captain	A sea captain who helps Viola
Valentine and Curio	Orsino's attendants
Priest	A Holy Father
Servant	Olivia's maid

SPROUTS FOR TWO

Brussels sprouts are not everyone's *plat du jour* at Christmas but if your folks insist that you have them, then why not suggest a game of Sprouts instead. Invented in 1967 by Princeton mathematician John H Conway and Michael S Paterson, while both were at the University of Cambridge, the rules of the game go:

1) Take a paper and pencil
2) Take two players
3) Draw a smallish number of dots on the paper – two is sufficient to start
4) Join two dots together or even one dot to itself in a circle – the line or circle must not touch or cross any other line or dot
5) Now place a new dot on the new line
6) Get your opponent to copy moves 4 and 5, taking it in turns after that
7) No dot can have more than three lines attached to it
8) You win if your opponent has no valid move – and vice-versa of course

Why 'Sprouts'? The lines sprout from the dots but the whole also resembles a sprout at the end – or after a few Christmas cocktails it will, but without the bitter aftertaste (unless you lose of course).

 Number of champagne brands tested in 2007 by Decanter *to find the best Christmas champagne – the winner was Waitrose own label*

DO THEY KNOW IT'S CHRISTMAS?

That was the question on everyone's lips in the winter of 1984 as Band Aid released their single of the same name on 3 December. The song 'Do They Know it's Christmas?' was penned by Bob Geldof and Midge Ure to help raise money for the 1984-5 famine in Ethiopia. Appearing on Richard Skinner's Radio 1 show, Geldof floated the idea of making a record to raise funds, and called for other musicians to be involved. A host of singers were soon volunteering, including Sting, Simon Le Bon, Bono, Paul Young, Paul Weller, George Michael, Tony Hadley, Phil Collins, Boy George and the girls from Bananarama. They recorded and mixed the single on 25-26 November (it took over 24 hours), singing the refrain 'Feed the world, let them know it's Christmas time' over and over again until everyone had the idea. The record went straight to number one, selling three million copies and raising millions of pounds for the cause. Every penny of the takings was donated to Ethiopia after Geldof demanded that Mrs Thatcher and her government waive the usual tax.

BEST-SELLING ALBUMS OF CHRISTMAS PAST – 2000s

From the British Library's Pop Goes the Library exhibition in association with The Official UK Charts Company, 26 July 2006 to 25 March 2007. More than 20% of albums are sold in December alone, many ending up in Christmas stockings.

2000	*1*	The Beatles
2001	*Swing When You're Winning*	Robbie Williams
2002	*Escapology*	Robbie Williams
2003	*Life for Rent*	Dido
2004	*Greatest Hits*	Robbie Williams
2005	*Curtain Call – The Hits*	Eminem
2006	*Beautiful World*	Take That
2007	*Spirit*	Leona Lewis

CHRISTMAS TRUCE TUNES

Songs or music videos that were inspired by the Christmas Truce of 1914, when the Germans and the French or British held a temporary festive ceasefire during World War I:

Tune	**By**
'Christmas 1914'	Mike Harding
'Christmas in the Trenches'	John McCutcheon
'Belleau Wood'	Garth Brooks
'Snoopy's Christmas'	The Royal Guardsmen
'All Together Now'	The Farm
'Pipes of Peace'	Paul McCartney

SANTA'S LITTLE HELPERS: KRAMPUS

Luckily for Santa, delivering all the presents at Christmas isn't just up to him and his tribe of elves and reindeer – a whole troop of gift-givers are out and about spreading their joy. As long as you've been a good little girl or boy, that is…

Perhaps one of the scariest of 'Santa's companions' – the present-day Krampus or 'Wilde Man' – is a pre-Christian traditional Alpine figure that survives in parts of Austria, Switzerland, Bavaria, Slovenia, Croatia and Hungary. He appears in a costume of red wooden mask (larve), black sheep's skin and horns. Much effort goes into the making of the masks – the scarier the better – as children and adults compete to come up with the most formidable creations. The word 'Krampus' comes from the Old High German word *krampen* meaning claw, and this adds to the macabre element of this helper. Traditionally, young men dress as the Krampus in the first two weeks of December, particularly on the evening of 5 December and roam the streets frightening children with their outfits plus rusty chains and bells. Some even run around with bunches of painted birch sticks or *virgács* used to taunt young females. Some parents also frighten their children by telling them they will get *virgács* instead of presents if they are naughty. Today, in Schladming, a town in Styria, Austria over 1,000 Krampus gather from all over the country to roam the streets. Women are advised not to go out on that night as they are popular targets for drunken Krampus and their overzealous *virgács*.

 Weight in Christmas puddings of CO_2 produced by average 2007 Christmas car travel, according to 'The Carbon Cost of Christmas' report

QUOTE UNQUOTE

Little Jack Horner sat in the corner,
Eating a Christmas pie.
He put in his thumb, and pulled out a plum,
And said, 'What a good boy am I?'
Traditional British nursery rhyme

THE NATIVITY: KING HEROD

Some things you may or may not know about principal characters in the Nativity:

- Herod I or Herod the Great was a Roman king of Judea, accepted to have lived between 73BC and 4BC, taking the throne in 43BC and elected as King of the Jews in 37BC when the Romans filly secured Judea
- Some details of his biography can be gleaned from the works of Josephus, a 1st-century Jewish historian
- In historic accounts Herod is known for his colossal building projects in Jerusalem, including the rebuilding of the Second Temple in Jerusalem, sometimes referred to as Herod's Temple
- In the Bible, Herod is known for the Massacre of the Innocents as described in the Gospel of St Matthew
- Shortly after the birth of Jesus, the Bible states that Magi from the East visited Herod to inquire the whereabouts of the child who was born King of the Jews. Herod was alarmed at a newborn king usurping his rule
- The Bible then says that Herod's advisers told him that a predicted 'anointed one' was to be born in Bethlehem. He sent the Magi there hoping that they would lead him to the child
- Matthew then tells us that when the Magi didn't return to tell him where the child was, Herod gave orders to kill all boys of the age of two and under in Bethlehem and its vicinity; Joseph, Mary and Baby Jesus fled to Egypt to stay there until Herod's death
- Disputes occur where historical accounts of Herod's life do not cite any Massacre of the Innocents or similar events as told in the Bible. However, history does chart Herod as being guilty of many brutal acts including the killing of his wife and two of his sons, and that he suffered throughout his lifetime from depression and paranoia

CHRISTMAS CRACKERS

The ones you wish you'd never pulled...

JOKE: What do angry mice send to each other at Christmas?

Answer on page 153

THE NIGHTMARE BEFORE CHRISTMAS... IN 60 SECONDS

A brief synopsis of the 1993 animated film The Nightmare Before Christmas, *so that you can get your fix of scary schmaltz at any time of year...*

The animated musical film *The Nightmare Before Christmas* was written and produced by Tim Burton, directed by Henry Selick and scored by the aptly named Danny Elfman. It follows a character called Jack Skellington, an undead skeleton, who is the leader of a holiday-themed world known as Halloween Town. In this magical world, strange creatures make plans for Halloween every year. Jack becomes bored of his repetitive lifestyle, and wandering into the hinterlands with his ghostly dog Zero, eventually stumbles upon the world of Christmas Town, a land of eternal winter. Jack becomes obsessed with Christmas and decides to usurp Sandy Claws (his mistaken name for Santa Claus). He assigns a task to every resident of Halloween Town, including Sally, a Frankenstein's monster of a rag doll who is secretly in love with Jack. The townsfolk start making gifts, which include man-eating wreaths, vampiric teddy bears, 30ft snakes and pull-string ducks with bloody bullet holes. Jack orders Lock, Stock and Barrel, a trio of child-like monsters to kidnap Sandy Claws and deliver him to the lair of Oogie Boogie, a gambling addict bogey man. When Jack attempts to deliver his presents to the children of the world, they are scared. The military is called out to capture him. They shoot him to the ground and he crawls into a cemetery, where he eventually wakes and realises that he can bring joy to the world in his own way by being ruler of just Halloween Town. He runs to Oogie Boogie's cave to find that Sally has tried to free Sandy Claws and has been captured too. Jack rescues them both and with Sandy Claws' help, kills Oogie Boogie. Santa delivers nice gifts to the children and gives the gift of snow to the people of Halloween Town. Sally and Jack finally get together. All is well in Halloween Town and Christmas goes on as usual.

 Distance in kilometres of the perimeter of Kiritimati, also known as Christmas Island, in the Indian Ocean

DURING THE COMPILATION OF THIS BOOK, THE COMPANION TEAM...

Saw nine ladies dancing, 10 lords a leaping, 11 pipers piping and a partridge in a pear tree.

Tried to be good but still got a piece of coal.

Left mince pies out for Santa and then crept down and ate them.

Made a drunken bet on a white Christmas and lost, again.

Finally took last year's Christmas tree to the dump, after six months.

Found out that eggnog isn't always the best hangover cure.

Took a spot of wassailing a little too far.

Got burnt lips while trying out a game of Snapdragon.

Swore that this would be the last time we would buy another set of fairy lights.

Argued about the theme for this year's Christmas tree.

Woke up with tinsel in our hair and glitter on our shoes.

Still couldn't resist another piece of chocolate orange.

Made a pledge to help 'Feed The World'.

Took heed from *A Christmas Carol* and tried not to be a Scrooge.

Sabotaged the cook's plans for a side order of sprouts.

Stood up for Santa against all those who says he doesn't exist.

Stuffed a turkey, stirred a pudding and found a sixpence.

Remembered *It's A Wonderful Life*.

Please note that although every effort has been made to ensure the accuracy of this book, the above facts may be the result of too much mulled wine, smoking bishop and brandy sauce.

Percentage increase of UK holidaymakers visiting Jordan at Christmas, according to the Association of British Travel Agents in 2005 151

'Ho, ho, ho!'
Santa Claus, universal gift giver

 Height, in feet, of the largest electric light Christmas tree in the world – the Zilker Christmas Tree in Austin, Texas, dating from the 1930s

CHRISTMAS CRACKERS

The answers. As if you needed them.

P12 The letter 'D'

P21 The Elf-abet

P31 He had low elf-esteem

P36 'I don't like sprouts'

P48 Claustrophobic

P55 The turkey – he's always stuffed

P60 'A merry Christmas to ewe'

P71 Ten: One to change the light bulb and nine to stand on each other's shoulders

P77 Mini vans

P89 No, he was elf-taught

P93 He had no body to go with

P101 Santa Paws

P107 Horn-aments

P120 Eight: One to screw in the light bulb and seven to hold Rudolph down

P129 Rude-olph

P136 'A furry merry Christmas and Happy mew year'

P143 Jungle bells, Jungle bells'

P150 Cross mouse cards

Distance, in miles southeast, of Christmas Island from Fanning, a coral atoll about seven miles in diameter

154 *DVD run time, in minutes, of the 1954 film* White Christmas, *starring Danny Kaye and Bing Crosby*

FURTHER READING

1001 Christmas Facts and Fancies
by Alfred Carl Hottes, De La Mare, 1937

A Christmas Book: An Anthology for Moderns
by DB Wyndham Lewis, JM Dent & Sons, 1928

A Christmas Carol
by Charles Dickens, Leipzig Bernh, Tachnitz June, 1843

A Christmas Garland
by Max Beerbohm, William Heinemann, 1912

A Holiday Book for Christmas and the New Year
by *Illustrated London News*, 1852

Advent and Christmas Wisdom
by GK Chesterton, Liguori Publications, 2007

Can Reindeer Fly? The Science of Christmas
by Roger Highfield, Phoenix, 2002

Christmas in England
by Washington Irving, GP Putnam, 1867

Christmas, Its Origins and Associations
by William Francis Dawson, Elliot Stock, 1902

Drinking With Dickens
by Cedric Dickens, New Amsterdam Books, 1990

Hercule Poirot's Christmas
by Agatha Christie, William Collins, 1938

The Adventure of the Christmas Pudding
by Agatha Christie, Collins, 1960

The Best of Mrs Beeton's Christmas
by Isabella Beeton, Weidenfeld & Nicolson, 2006

The Father Christmas Letters
by JRR Tolkien, Allen and Unwin, 1976

156 *Number of days before Christmas that the annual World Congress of Santas began in Bakken, Denmark, in 2002*

ACKNOWLEDGEMENTS

We gratefully acknowledge permission to reprint extracts of copyright material in this book from the following authors, publishers and executors:

The Letters of Father Christmas, JRR Tolkien
© The JRR Tolkien Copyright Trust 1999, 2004.
Published by kind permission of Harper Collins Publishers Ltd.

Christmas Holiday, W Somerset Maugham
Reprinted by kind permission of The Random House Group Ltd and AP Watt Ltd.

Cider with Rosie, Laurie Lee
Published by Hogarth Press. Reprinted by kind permission of The Random House Group Ltd.

Holidays in Hell, PJ O'Rourke
© 1988 by PJ O'Rourke. Reprinted by kind permission of Grove/Atlantic, Inc. and Macmillan Publishers Ltd.

INDEX